TRAINING FOR LEADERSHIP

TRAINING FOR LEADERSHIP

JOHN ADAIR

GOWER PRESS

First published in Great Britain 1968 by
Macdonald and Company (Publishers) Limited

Reprinted 1978, 1979 by Gower Press, Teakfield Limited,
Westmead, Farnborough, Hampshire, England

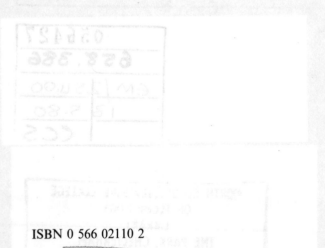

ISBN 0 566 02110 2

Printed in Great Britain by Biddles Ltd, Guildford, Surrey

To
My Father and Mother
and Mary

CONTENTS

PREFACE

'Smith is not a born leader yet,' wrote one despairing manager upon a junior's report. What can either he or Smith do about it? Can leadership potential be developed?

This is an important question for two reasons. Because of a variety of factors men and women are coming to expect a much higher standard of leadership than their fathers and mothers enjoyed or endured. Secondly, there is a widespread feeling, both in this country and beyond the seas, that the number of 'born leaders' falls far short of the requirement for good leadership.

The aim of this book is to demonstrate that leadership potential can indeed be developed in more effective ways than at present and to show how this may be done.

Although these pages contain many examples drawn from the military field, the book as a whole is not primarily concerned with any one form or manifestation of leadership. It so happens that the approach described below received its first thorough testing in the officer training schools of the armed services, but the understanding of leadership, the educational principles and methods for developing it, are equally relevant in other fields. Chapters 7 and 8 describe, for instance, the shape this author's approach to leadership training has already taken in some management development programmes. Many other industrial firms, several management training centres, including university departments, and a number of public services, such as the police and the fire services, are now considering how best to apply the same approach in their own particular situations.

Many of my friends and colleagues have placed me in their debt by commenting upon the manuscript of this book. For this service I offer my warmest thanks to Major-General Peter Hunt,

9

Professor Kenneth Ingham, Air Commodore Neil Cameron, Mr John Garnett, Mr Bernard Babington Smith, Mr Jerry Pink, Colonel Dennis O'Flaherty, Mr Anthony Brett-James, Mr Andrew Forrest, Captain Susan Greenslade, the Reverend Dr Peter Rudge and the Reverend John Arnold. Space does not allow me to thank all those, besides the above, who have contributed to its contents.

The staff of the Central Library at Sandhurst have earned my gratitude by their consistent helpfulness over many months. Lastly, I must thank Mrs Rose Hance for typing the numerous drafts of the manuscript, and Mrs Mary Russell for proof-reading the final one.

CHAPTER ONE

THE NATURE OF LEADERSHIP

Before the training of leaders can be discussed we must first review the different assumptions and theories upon which it might be based.

The method adopted in this chapter is to look first at perhaps the oldest and most widely held general idea that leaders are 'born not made'. From this point we shall trace the evolution of research upon the subject, sticking as closely as possible to the main highway.

The Qualities Approach

'Leaders are born not made.' This is perhaps the most common assumption about leadership. Those who hold it maintain that there are certain inborn qualities, such as initiative, courage, intelligence and humour, which together predestine a man to be a leader. By the exercise of will-power, itself seen as an important leadership trait, or by the rough tutorship of experience, some of these qualities might be developed. But the essential pattern is given at birth.

Although there is a positive contribution to our understanding of leadership latent in this *qualities approach*, it suffers from several disadvantages as far as training for leadership is concerned. The first of these drawbacks is that no one has yet been able to discover any agreement upon what are these qualities, which will give a man dominion over his fellows in any situation in which he finds himself. One survey of 20 experimental studies, made in 1940, revealed that only five per cent of the leadership qualities examined were common to four or more studies.[1] In fact there are a bewildering number of trait names which the professional or amateur student might use to make up his portfolio.

The writers of one article have listed 17,000 words used to describe qualities of personality.[2] Although there has been a continual effort to boil down the qualities to those which are essential, lengthy lists are still common. Until 1958 Eaton Hall Officer Cadet Training Unit issued one which contained 32 qualities, and at one military conference the author was handed a list of 64 leadership traits! The reader may check this lack of agreement by turning to Appendix A on page 141 where he may compare for himself the lists of leadership traits advocated by various armed services in the western world.

You will notice that 'courage' and 'initiative' appear in most columns in Appendix A. Do they form the core of military leadership? But, we may reflect, *all* soldiers, regardless of rank, need to be brave and resourceful. So by isolating those two qualities we are no nearer to understanding the mystery of leadership. Indeed there are plenty of examples of soldiers who possess both courage and initiative, but who by no stretch of the imagination could be called leaders.

Besides this lack of consensus as to what are the qualities of leadership, there is a second major disadvantage to this theory. The qualities approach is ill-suited to act as a basis for leadership training. Intrinsically it hardly favours the idea of training at all, and instead encourages a concentration on selection. The ability to recognize a born leader becomes all important, and attempts to 'make' leaders are viewed with suspicion.

In fact, how could the 'qualities of leadership' be used in training? The teacher or instructor might speak in the language of traits to the student, but it is difficult for the latter to know what to *do* with such remarks. If told, for example, that he lacks a sense of humour—how does he develop it? By reading *Punch* every week? No, there is nothing more serious than a young man bent on improving his sense of humour, and nothing more self-centred than this cultivation of one's own personality. And in the long run self-centredness is the one certain disqualification for any form of leadership. At the worst an unskilful teacher, using the 'qualities of leadership' language, can do incalculable harm. A comment such as 'Jones, you lack moral fibre' may take away from Jones even that self-confidence which he had.

One usually finds that students who have attempted a self-development based on the traits approach have abandoned it after a few weeks, either in despair because they have not attained the desired qualities or (much worse) in pride because they believe they have. The pattern is often that followed by an Eaton Hall officer cadet known to the author, who resolved to practise 1–5 on the issued list of 32 'leadership qualities' on Mondays, 6–10 on Tuesdays, 11–15 on Wednesdays, etc. By Friday he had completely forgotten Monday's quota, and had become so dispirited that he abandoned the Herculean task. (Such schemes for moral self-improvement, however, if persisted in, are seldom wasted. The lives of the saints illustrate the point that when these struggles are abandoned and become hidden in a person's life, they may then bear—much later—the fruit of character.)

Therefore the qualities assumption does not form a good basis for leadership training programmes. But it does have other uses. First, it reminds us that natural potential for leadership varies in individuals. Secondly, many of us need the language of qualities to transfer our knowledge of a person's leadership ability to someone else. Thirdly, this approach emphasises the importance of what the leader *is* as a person, in an age which may be inclined temperamentally to skate over the importance of character as opposed to personality. Certainly we need more research into the qualities understanding of leadership, but until this is carried out there is no reason to make it the main basis for a training course.

The Situational Approach

Besides revealing the inadequacies of the traits analysis of leadership the social scientists investigating the subject in the late 1940's began to underline the importance of the situation in determining who would become a leader in a given group. R. M. Stogdill, for example, who studied the evidence for 29 qualities appearing in 124 studies, concluded that although intelligence, scholarliness, dependability, social participation, and socio-economic status were found to bear some relation to leadership,

> ... the evidence suggests that leadership is a relationship that exists between persons in a social situation, and that persons who are leaders in one situation may not necessarily be leaders in other situations.[3]

This finding expressed what might be called a *situational approach* to leadership, namely that the man who becomes (or should become) the leader in a group depends upon the particular

13

task, the organisational and the environmental setting. Another study by W. O. Jenkins, published a year earlier in 1947, supports this conclusion. After reviewing 74 studies on military leadership the author wrote :

> Leadership is specific to the particular situation under investigation. Who becomes the leader of a particular group engaging in a particular activity and what the leadership characteristics are in the given case are a function of the specific situation ... [there are] wide variations in the characteristics of individuals who become leaders in similar situations and even great divergence in leadership behaviour in different situations ... The only common factor appeared to be that leaders in a particular field need and tend to possess superior general or technical competence or knowledge in that area. General intelligence does not seem to be the answer ... [4]

To illustrate this theory let us imagine some shipwreck survivors on a tropical island. The soldier in the party might take command if natives attacked them, the builder lead during the work of erecting houses, and the farmer might direct the labour of growing food. In other words, leadership would pass from member to member according to the situation. 'Situation' in this context means primarily the task of the group.

There are two drawbacks to this approach as far as training leaders is concerned. First, it is unsatisfactory in most organisations for leadership to change hands in this manner. At one time the Royal Air Force veered towards this doctrine by entertaining the idea that if a bomber crashed in a jungle the officer who took command for the survival operation might not be captain of the aircraft but the man most qualified for the job. But role flexibility to this degree tends to create more problems than it solves.

Secondly, an explanation was needed for the fact that certain men seemed to possess a general leadership competence which enabled them to exercise an influence over their fellows in a whole range of situations. Of course, the compilers of trait lists had been seeking, without much success, to analyse this general aptitude, and there was no denying its reality. Even so, by seeing leadership not as a quality but as a relationship, and by grasping the importance of the leader possessing the appropriate technical or professional knowledge required in the given situation, the proponents of this approach made a most valuable contribution to our understanding of the subject.

The Functional Approach

So far the research work described has been largely literary: the analysis and comparison of books and articles on leadership. In the late 1930's, however, more objective research commenced into the behaviour of actual small groups both in what were described as 'laboratory' conditions and also 'in the field', in an attempt to bring the scientific methods of observation, hypothesis and verification by experiment to bear upon the phenomena of social life.

These studies have produced a vast crop of papers on the social psychology of small groups, including the leadership displayed in them. From this wealth the author selected one general theory which might be called 'the theory of group needs', as having the greatest potential relevance to leadership training. By combining and developing this theory with the positive contributions of the two earlier and complementary approaches— qualities and situational—he produced a comprehensive and integrated understanding of leadership. To grasp 'functional leadership', as this approach came to be called, it is necessary first to look at the concept of 'group needs'.

If we look closely at any working group we may become aware of its distinctive corporate life, its difference from others even in the same organisation. Upon the analogy with individual human beings this could be called the 'group personality'. But, according to the theory of group needs, just as individuals differ in many ways and yet share certain common attributes and needs, so also do the corporate entities or social organisms which we know as groups. Let us now examine the most important of these group needs.

With reference to working groups, the most obvious group need is to achieve the common *task*. Generally speaking, all such groups come together consciously or unconsciously because the individuals in them cannot alone fulfil an objective. For example, one man by himself could not climb Mount Everest and survive; therefore a team is assembled for the job and co-operation becomes essential.

But does the group as a whole experience the need to the task within the natural time limits for it? Now a r very aware of his need for food if he is well-fed, and so one would expect a group to be relatively oblivious of any sense of need if its task is being successfully performed. In this case the only sign of a need having been met is the satisfaction or elation which overtake the group in its moments of triumph, a happiness which social man may count among his deepest joys.

Before such a fulfilment, however, many groups pass through a 'black night of despair' when it may appear that the group will be compelled to disperse without achieving what it set out to do. If the members are not committed to the common goal this will be a comparatively painless event; but if they are, the group will exhibit various degrees of anxiety and frustration. Scapegoats for the corporate failure may be chosen and punished; reorganisations might take place and new leaders emerge. Thus adversity reveals the nature of group life more clearly than prosperity. In it we may see signs or symptoms of the need to get on effectively with whatever the group has come together to do.

Secondly, in order to achieve the common objective the group must work as a team. Therefore it needs to be maintained as a cohesive unity. This is not so easy to perceive as the task need; like an iceberg, much of the life of any group lies below the surface. The distinction that the task need concerns things and the second need involves people does not help overmuch. Again, it is best to think of groups which are threatened without by forces aimed at their disintegration or within by disruptive people or ideas. We can then see how they give priority to maintaining themselves against these external or internal pressures, sometimes showing great ingenuity in the process. Many of the written or unwritten rules of the group are designed to promote this unity and to maintain cohesiveness at all costs. Those who rock the boat, or infringe group standards and corporate balance, may expect reactions varying from friendly indulgence to downright anger. Instinctively a common feeling exists that 'united we stand, divided we fall', that good relationships, desirable in themselves, are also essential means towards the shared end. This need to create and promote group cohesiveness we may call the *team-maintenance* need.

The third area of need present in the corporate life inheres in the individual members rather than in the group itself. To the latter they bring a variety of needs—physical, social and vocational—which may or may not be met by participating in the activity of the group. Probably physical needs first drew men to-gether in working groups : the primitive hunter could take away from the slain elephant a hunk of meat and a piece of hide for his own family. Nowadays the means for satisfying these basic needs of food, shelter and protection are received in money rather than in kind, but the principle remains the same.

There are, however, other needs less tangible or conscious even to their possessors which the social interaction of working to-gether in groups may or may not fulfil. These tend to merge into each other, and they cannot be isolated with any precision, but the list below will indicate their character. Drawn from the work of A. H. Maslow[5] it also makes the point that needs are organised on a priority basis. As basic needs become relatively satisfied the higher needs come to the fore and become motivating influences.[6]

Basic Physiologi-cal Needs 1st	Safety Needs 2nd	Social Needs 3rd	Self-esteem Needs 4th	Self-realization Needs 5th
Hunger Thirst Sleep etc.	Security Protection from danger	Belonging Social activity Love	Self-respect Status Recognition	Growth Personal development Accomplishment

1. THE PRIORITY OF NEEDS

These needs spring from the depths of our common life as human beings. They may attract us to, or repel us from, any given group. Underlying them all is the fact that people need each other, not just to survive but to achieve and develop personality. This growth occurs in a whole range of social activity —friendship, marriage, neighbourhood—but inevitably work groups are extremely important because so many people spend so much of their waking time in them.

These three areas of need cannot be studied in watertight compartments : each exerts an influence for good or ill upon the others. Thus we may visualise the needs as three overlapping circles :

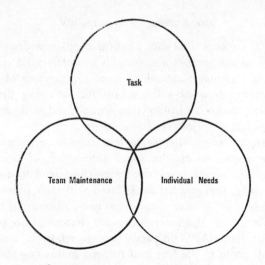

2. INTER-ACTION OF GROUP NEEDS

If you place a penny over the 'Task' circle it will immediately cover segments of the other two circles as well. In other words, lack of task or failure to achieve it will affect both team maintenance, e.g. increasing disruptive tendencies, and also the area of individual needs, lowering member satisfaction within the group. Move the penny on to the 'Team Maintenance' circle, and again the impact of a near-complete lack of relationships in the group on both task and individual needs may be seen at a glance.

Conversely, when a group achieves its task the degree of group cohesiveness and enjoyment of membership should go up. Morale, both corporate and individual, will be higher. And if the members of a group happen to get on extremely well together and find that they can work closely as a team, this will increase their work performance and also meet some important needs which individuals bring with them into the common life.

These three interlocking circles therefore illustrate the general point that each area of need exerts an influence upon the other two; they do not form watertight compartments.

Clearly, in order that the group should fulfil its task and be held together as a working team, certain functions will have to be performed. By 'function' in this context we mean any behaviour, words or actions which meet one or more spheres of the group needs, or *areas of leadership responsibility* as they may also be called. Defining the aim, planning, and encouraging the group, are examples of what is meant by the word 'function'. (See Appendix D for other examples.)

18

In most small groups the responsibility for the performance of such functions rests with the designated leader, though this is not to say that he is expected to perform them all himself. Nor can we assert that there are certain functions which must always be supplied, for this depends upon the situation in the widest sense, including the task and the nature of the group.

By contrast with the traditional view that a leader possesses certain traits or qualities which make him stand out in any company, the functional approach stresses that leadership is essentially an interaction between leader, group members and the situation. Yet the personality of the leader is not ignored in this functional approach. It may often serve the group by representing the qualities valued both for corporate survival and the completion of the task. Thus an army officer ought to possess courage, the cardinal military virtue, although this will not in itself make him a leader. Perhaps Sir Winston Churchill in the war years afforded the supreme example in our time of the 'representative function of character', as it could be called. His bull-dog demeanour and resolute speech personified the spirit of a nation, just as surely as did the youthful vigour of President Kennedy represent the mighty energies of the United States in our own day. Still, the functional approach lays emphasis not upon what the leader *is* in terms of traits, or upon what he *knows* of the appropriate technical knowledge, but upon his ability to provide the necessary functions in a manner acceptable to the group, i.e. what he actually *does* to lead in response to the three over-lapping areas of task, team maintenance and individual needs.

The question of how far the designated leader should share his leadership functions with group members deserves consideration. Not many leaders consciously think this problem out; most accept the assumptions on the matter prevalent in their organisation although in some cases these are ripe for review. Supposing, however, that a leader became aware that there were alternative patterns from which he could choose, what would be the factors that he should consider before determining upon one or other of them?

In a thoughtful answer to this question two writers in the *Harvard Business Review*[7] have suggested three : the leader himself, his subordinates and the situation. Let us look at each of these in turn :

The Leader

The personality of the designated leader—his interests, aptitudes and temperament—will exert an influence on the pattern of shared leadership in any group. His 'doctrine of man', as the theologians would say, determines much. If he regards people as things to be used for his own ends, pawns on the chessboard, then he will not see much need for consultation. If he is temperamentally lazy, then he may well allow group members a greater share in leadership functions than either their experience or the requirements of the situation dictate.

Perhaps the critical factor in the temperament of the leader is the degree to which he feels secure in an uncertain situation. 'The manager who releases control over the decision-making process thereby reduces the predictability of the outcome. Some managers have a greater need than others for predictability and stability in their environment. This "tolerance of ambiguity" is being viewed increasingly by psychologists as a key variable in a person's manner of dealing with problems.'[8]

'Know thyself,' enjoins the Greek philosopher. By looking at his own experience, the reactions of others to himself, and the comments of friends, the leader should gain a modicum of self-knowledge. He should be aware of any bias in his character; for example, whether or not he tends to be too task-centred and correspondingly less conscious of the needs of individuals, or whether he operates most efficiently and effectively in one pattern of shared functions rather than another. The end of such study is more appropriate action. Like a marksman archer 'aiming off' into the wind, a leader can then make allowances for these unseen tendencies in his character when he perceives that a particular situation demands a different kind of response from his normal one. Although he may feel it 'unnatural' to share out or arrogate to himself leadership functions (as the case may be) this will not be the judgment of others if he has appreciated the situation correctly.

The Subordinates

The obvious question here for the leader to ask himself is how far the group members possess the necessary knowledge, experience and skill relevant to the problem in hand to participate satisfactorily in leadership functions. At one end of the scale a class of junior school-children clearly lack the qualifications to decide how they are going to plan out their work; it has to be done for them by the adult leader. On the other hand, a team of highly skilled technicians will not require this degree of 'spoon feeding' on how to tackle a common task; the steps may become evident to all of them at once. The leader therefore should take into account the degree of 'expert' knowledge, experience and social skill resident in the group as the second main factor in his appreciation.

One note of caution, however, should be sounded at this point. Some leaders rationalise their temperamental preference for a pattern by claiming that 'their' group is incapable of being more than submissive or dependent followers. In those cases the leaders concerned lack sufficient self-knowledge to discern their own guiding motives. In fact it is rarely true that a group is so devoid in all three respects of any leadership potential that one man or woman must do it all for them; this is sometimes a fiction created as a piece of self-justification by a domineering personality. Moreover, entrusting the inexperienced with a share in leadership functions is often the only way of giving them the necessary experience, and of motivating them to acquire the appropriate knowledge and skill. There is nothing more mysterious and exciting than this ability of good leaders to transform their followers : without it, a vital element, the light and life of leadership, is missing. The great leader is always aware of latent powers in people which can be evoked and harnessed : he responds to these like a gold-diviner, thereby meeting an important segment of individual needs. Generally speaking, the more members participate in decisions, the more they feel motivated to carry them out; and the more they share in the life of the group in this way, the more chance there is that their potentialities as persons will be fulfilled.

The Situation

There are, however, limits to which the leader can go in this educative process without a denial of his own responsibility, and these are set by the situation. 'Situation' in this context must again be understood in a wide sense, embracing group task and the working environment. When we think of an important (predominantly) task function such as decision-making, it is clear that in certain situations life or death may depend upon the speed of a group's reaction. In such cases it is appropriate for the leader to retain or concentrate authority in his own hands rather than share it with the group. In fact some research shows that in hastily formed groups responding to crisis situations, for example serious motor accidents and forest fires, not only is a strong authoritative leadership tolerated from one man, but it is also positively expected.

Consequently, we shall not be surprised to find that groups which habitually, or characteristically, operate in crisis situations exhibit a certain pattern of leadership, with the designated leader in a fixed position of authority, and followers trained and disciplined to obey his orders promptly and without discussion. Obvious examples of such groups would include military platoons, the crews of airliners, ships' crews and operating theatre teams. But the stress element is not solely related to life-and-death; sometimes decisions must be taken promptly in order to avoid great loss to an industrial company. Time limits may not always allow the manager to share his decision-making functions with his subordinates.

Although the characteristic situation influences the general pattern it does not arbitrarily fix it on a given point. The platoon commander, for example, in barracks and on peace-time exercises will act towards his men in such a way as not to betray the residual authority he needs to command on active service, but he would be unwise to behave in those situations as if a fierce battle were raging about his ears. There is a flexibility within any pattern which the good leader will exploit according to the *specific* situation without detriment to his prime responsibility in the *characteristic* one. Indeed, a chairman of a committee may range widely with an appropriate pattern during the confines of a two-hour meeting, or even within the context of five minutes.

A Decision-making Continuum

The *Harvard Business Review* article already mentioned contains a useful diagram showing the full range of sharing which might take place in any group over the general function of decision-making :

Manager makes decision and announces it	Manager 'sells' decision	Manager presents ideas and invites questions	Manager presents tentative decision subject to change	Manager presents problem, gets suggestions, makes decision	Manager defines limits, asks group to make decision	Manager permits subordinates to function within limits defined by superior

3. A DECISION-MAKING CONTINUUM

This is largely self-explanatory. It should not be supposed, however, that the points between which a leader habitually acts on this scale necessarily describe the degree of shared *leadership* in a group. Decision-making in the sense meant by the authors is but one task function, albeit a key one. We could equally well construct diagrams to illustrate the amount of member involvement in team maintenance functions. Indeed, very often a leader who exercises virtually all the task functions himself will delegate (or be expected to share) many team-maintenance functions to other members of the group. In an infantry platoon, for example, the platoon sergeant often responds to the other two areas of need, holding the men together and making sure that they get food and mail where possible. In less formal groups, a factory production team, for example, those sharing in leadership in this way may not be designated, but nevertheless they will act to complement the functions performed by the appointed leader. As a general principle, in any group larger than 7 or 8 members, some degree of sharing becomes essential : there are so many functions required for the group to work effectively on the task without losing cohesion and without individual needs being overlooked that the designated leader cannot supply them all himself, and he must therefore delegate some of them to others.

Conclusion

In 1952 C. A. Gibb concluded an extensive survey of research into the subject by stating that 'any comprehensive theory of leadership must incorporate and integrate all of the major variables which are now known to be involved, namely (1) the personality of the leader, (2) the followers with their attitudes, needs and problems, (3) the group itself ... (4) the situations as determined by physical setting, nature of task etc ... No really satisfactory theoretical formulation is yet available.'[9] In this chapter the simple concept of 'functional leadership' has been outlined not so much to meet the academic need mentioned by Gibb but to serve as a basis for more effective leadership training.

Although 'theorising about' and 'analysing' a subject like leadership which will always transcend even the most comprehensive description may not appeal to many readers, it has been a necessary labour. For if we are not clear upon the meaning of leadership it is impossible to design an effective training programme.

CHAPTER TWO

LOOKING AT LEADERS

This chapter is in fact a 'pocket anthology' mainly of descriptions
of actual leaders in concrete historical situations. The reader is
invited to study them, however, bearing in mind the *functional*
concept of leadership described in Chapter 1. It is hoped that he
will find that this theory illumines these practical examples, that
it becomes easier to *see* leadership and to understand why a
particular individual was successful as a leader. After he has
completed this chapter, the reader may have been able to clothe
with flesh-and-blood the rather abstract and analytical ideas
of Chapter 1.

Not all the extracts are descriptions of leaders. Some have been
chosen because they contain the thoughts of a proven leader upon
the group or the situation in which he exercised his responsibility.
The theme of the anthology is the relation of the leader to other
members of his team in the context of a common task, and therefore general quotations about leadership, or the mere listing of
'qualities', have been omitted in favour of concrete examples of
how leaders think and act in order to attain the task, build and
foster team maintenance, and meet the needs of individual
members.

The fact that more than half of the extracts refer to leaders in
military situations is not significant. It is largely due to the fact
that descriptions of military leadership tend to appear in print
more often than, for example, those of individual industrial
leaders at work. The *underlying* principles of leadership are the
same. Indeed it could be argued that the crisis element of war
serves to reveal the essential nature of leadership more clearly.
This does not mean, of course, that the applied form or pattern
of leadership necessary in a military situation will be transferable

25

to any other setting. Here it is sufficient for the reader to identify the main areas of need present in a group as depicted in the three over-lapping circles on page 18, and to distinguish the key functions performed by leaders to meet them effectively.

Gino Watkins

Gino Watkins led expeditions to Edge Island (near Spitzbergen), Labrador and Greenland. This extract from J. M. Scott's biography concerns his leadership in Greenland during 1930. The average age of the 14 members of the party was 25 years old, eighteen months more than Watkins. He died in 1933, drowned in a Greenland lake while out hunting in a kayak. Posthumously he was awarded the Polar Medal with Arctic clasp.

As quietly as if it had been a Scottish shooting-party Gino had organised the greatest British expedition to the Arctic for half a century, and he was carrying it through in the same unofficial, unheroic spirit ... When he sailed for Edge Island he had no first-hand knowledge of the conditions. He was successful because he could sum up positions quickly and act without hesitation, and he was a tactful and popular leader because he asked the opinions of the members of the party who had each some special knowledge to impart. In Labrador it had been the same. Everyone he came in contact with was gratified by his respectful interest in all they said and, without fully realising it, they did what he wanted them to do and taught him all the useful knowledge they possessed. In England he had read widely and had asked pertinent questions whenever he met well-travelled men, so that by now he knew a great deal about polar technique; and although he was no scientist he understood clearly enough what the specialists were after ...

He did what he enjoyed and visited the places that he wanted to visit, but, being there, he used all the resources in his power to bring back everything he could. By knowledge he was best qualified to lead in Greenland quite apart from the fact that he had created the expedition. Most of the party had seen little of him before they sailed, and they were ready to treat him at least with the outward deference they were accustomed to show to a commander. If he had enjoyed that sort of thing he could very easily have kept it up. But his sense of humour made it absurd. He took trouble to climb down from this uncomfortable eminence by telling stories against himself, flirting with the Eskimos, posing as an utter Philistine or joining in every menial task . . .

Besides, he gave himself no privileges at all. His bed was no more comfortable than ours; probably it was less so, judging by the dog harness and rifles which were piled on top of it. His clothes were no better and his private possessions far less numerous. His dogs I had given to him after selecting what I considered the best team for myself. Only his native hunting instruments were superior because he had taken great trouble in acquiring them. I was reminded that once in Labrador I heard a man call him Boss, and Gino had been a little embarrassed and very much amused. That was not his name, so why address him so?

As unemotionally as one is conscious of a fact of life, he knew that he would lead in any circumstance. Neither familiarity nor conventional discipline could alter that, and he preferred familiarity because he had no wish to be lonely. He was a young man who set out to enjoy himself and to make others enjoy themselves as well, because he believed that people work better when they are happy.

All that was comparatively easy. Almost anybody with a sense of humour could have done as much if his sole object was to be accepted as a member of the party. But to one who was responsible for making people do unpleasant tasks it was a self-imposed handicap which could only be overcome by a very high type of personality. There could be no bluffing in such leadership; it would either prove magnetic by its inspiring originality or lead to chaos by its non-existence.

At first there was some argument as to Gino's wisdom in following the course which he had chosen. People like the Bedouin are used to such methods : they expect a leader to be one of themselves and recognise a strong character most easily in contrast to circumstances which they themselves experience . . . One or two of the Service men in particular were upset by the apparently casual suggestions which passed for commands. Gino said it was absurd to write to a man you could talk to; but even so, they would have appreciated the comfortable definiteness of written orders, if only to assure them that they had done all that was expected. Others, although they could not have admitted it, had looked for something more in exploration : a consciousness of adventure and romance. All this was so straightforward and matter-of-fact that if one so much as grew a beard one felt theatrical. Gino's plans and his rebellious why-not? points of view were exciting enough if one could swallow them; but without experience we had no personal standard to judge by; and could anyone so casual have taken trouble to prepare the best equipment?

As time passed and experience brought knowledge, these doubts were laid one after another. It very soon became apparent that the equipment was extraordinarily good. The clothing was light and warm, while the sledging rations – Gino's most striking innovation – were excellent; no one had been really hungry on any journey and there had only been one serious case of frostbite. The sledging tents, lighter and easier to pitch then the older Antarctic models, had withstood considerable storms. The dome-shaped tent at the ice-cap station, which was designed somewhat on the lines of an Eskimo igloo with a tunnel entrance and small tube ventilator at the apex, had so far proved efficient, though it had not yet had to withstand the hardest test of all. The Base hut, with its double walls and central kitchen, was warm and well designed. These facts and a thousand little things bore proof of care and foresight.

The work of the first season proved remarkably successful. Luck played a part, as in the absence of heavy ice at Kangerdlugsuak, but luck is a valuable addition to a leader's reputation. In detail the journeys had not developed exactly as expected; but the acting leaders, unrestricted by precise directions yet understanding very clearly the general objective, had used their initiative to achieve a useful end. In the course of our work we had done things that we had never done before – we had driven dogs and navigated small boats through ice – and we had found these things remarkably easy. Knowing that so much had depended upon ourselves, our self-confidence increased and with it our confidence in Gino; for his plans were only alarming when we doubted our ability to fulfil our part in them. Having discovered the surprising fact that we were as good men as Gino thought we were, we accepted him as a splendid leader. He was exacting, he was ruthlessly indifferent to small discomforts like cold or unvaried fresh meat diets at the Base, he was disconcerning in his words and actions, but he would never be at a loss and would never blame. Once only Gino remarked that a man was beginning to behave badly and that he thought he would have to have a row with him. He had his row, in a roaring temper, so it seemed, and afterwards they were far stronger friends than they had been before.

If he told inexperienced men to do what they thought best, and if they made some fatal blunder, the responsibility would be his just as surely as if he had expressly ordered that disastrous action. The world would see it thus and so would he. It was a risky policy, but for his purpose the risk was unavoidable.

Briefly, his method of leadership was to train each man to be a leader: his ideal exploring party consisted of nothing else. These were young men and he was looking ahead towards other, more perplexing, quests.

In Gino's opinion, initiative and self-confidence were all-important and so he would keep nobody in leading-strings. The boy who stood on the burning deck seemed to him nothing but a fool. Once, too, he had gone to a film about the sinking of a great liner. When he saw the last brave men, who had put the women and children in the only boats, standing at attention to sing, 'Nearer, my God, to Thee,' he turned to his neighbour in the darkness and in an urgent whisper said, 'Why the hell don't they build rafts instead of wasting their time being heroic?' From the same coldly practical point of view he had told me on our last journey that if the food ran out and he himself should die he would naturally expect to be eaten; and, when I demurred, he added, 'Well, I'd eat you, but then, of course, you are much more fat and appetising.' . . .

He did not preach this philosophy which I have attempted to explain. He followed the path which he had chosen, enjoying every step, quick to shock, slow to offend, but caring nothing how his words and actions were interpreted when he felt their aim was right, leading without looking back because he knew that we would follow him. Both as a friend and a leader he had always something in reserve, some depth which gave occasional proof of its existence, but which even he did not understand. The one aspect aroused interest and the other confidence.

Field Marshal Lord Slim

In this chapter from 'Defeat into Victory' Lord Slim describes how he analysed his responsibilities as a leader in a given situation, and then carried them out. Of particular interest is the way in which his appreciation and action covers comprehensively the task, team maintenance and individual needs of a great army. Lord Slim saw from the outset that it was necessary for the leader to explain not only 'how' the aim is to be achieved, but also 'why', and this he did by relating objectives to larger purposes. The passage illustrates most clearly the inter-relation of the three areas, and how the leader went about providing the necessary functions effectively.

So when I took command, I sat quietly down to work out this business of morale. I came to certain conclusions, based not on any theory that I had studied, but on some experience and a good deal of hard thinking. It was on these conclusions that I set out consciously to raise the fighting spirit of my army.

Morale is a state of mind. It is that intangible force which will move a whole group of men to give their last ounce to achieve something, without counting the cost to themselves; that makes them feel they are part of something greater than themselves. If they are to feel that, their morale must, if it is to endure—and the essence of morale is that it should endure —have certain foundations. These foundations are spiritual, intellectual, and material, and that is the order of their importance. Spiritual first, because only spiritual foundations can stand real strain. Next intellectual, because men are swayed by reason as well as feeling. Material last—important, but last —because the very highest kinds of morale are often met when material conditions are lowest.

I remember sitting in my office and tabulating these foundations of morale something like this :

1. *Spiritual*
   (a) There must be a great and noble object.
   (b) Its achievement must be vital.
   (c) The method of achievement must be active, aggressive.
   (d) The man must feel that what he is and what he does matters directly towards the attainment of the object.
2. *Intellectual*
   (a) He must be convinced that the object can be

obtained; that it is not out of reach.

(b) He must see, too, that the organization to which he belongs and which is striving to attain the object is an efficient one.

(c) He must have confidence in his leaders and know that whatever dangers and hardships he is called upon to suffer, his life will not be lightly flung away.

3. *Material*

(a) The man must feel that he will get a fair deal from his commanders and from the army generally.

(b) He must, as far as humanly possible, be given the best weapons and equipment for his task.

(c) His living and working conditions must be made as good as they can be.

It was one thing thus neatly to marshal my principles but quite another to develop them, apply them, and get them recognized by the whole army.

At any rate, our spiritual foundation was a firm one. I use the word spiritual, not in its strictly religious meaning, but as belief in a cause . . .

We had this; and we had the advantage over our enemies that ours was based on real, not false, spiritual values. If ever an army fought in a just cause we did. We coveted no man's country; we wished to impose no form of government on any nation. We fought for the clean, the decent, the free things of life, for the right to live our lives in our own way as others could live theirs, to worship God in what faith we chose, to be free in body and mind, and for our children to be free. We fought only because the powers of evil had attacked these things. No matter what the religion or race of any man in the Fourteenth Army, he *must* feel this, feel that he had indeed a worthy cause, and that if he did not defend it life would not be worth living for him or for his children. Nor was it enough to have a worthy cause. It must be positive, aggressive, not a mere passive, defensive, anti-something feeling. So our object became not to defend India, to stop the Japanese advance, or even to occupy Burma, but to destroy the Japanese Army, to smash it as an evil thing.

The fighting soldier facing the enemy can see that what he does, whether he is brave or craven, matters to his comrades and directly influences the result of the battle. It is harder for the

31

man working on the road far behind, the clerk checking stores in a dump, the headquarter's telephone operator monotonously plugging through his calls, the sweeper carying out his menial tasks, the quartermaster's orderly issuing bootlaces in a reinforcement camp—it is hard for these and a thousand others to see that they too matter. Yet every one of the half-million in the army—and it was many more later—had to be made to see where his task fitted into the whole, to realize what depended on it, and to feel pride and satisfaction in doing it well.

Now these things, while the very basis of morale, because they were purely matters of feeling and emotion, were the most difficult to put over, especially to the British portion of the army. The problem was how to instil or revive their beliefs in the men of many races who made up the Fourteenth Army. I felt there was only one way to do it, by a direct approach to the individual men themselves. Not by written exhortations, by wireless speeches, but by informal talks and contacts between troops and commanders. There was nothing new in this; my corps and divisional commanders and others right down the scale were already doing it. It was the way we had held the troops together in the worst days of the 1942 retreat; we remained an army then only because the men saw and knew their commanders. All I did now was to encourage my commanders to increase these activities, unite them in a common approach to the problem, in the points that they would stress, and in the action they would take to see that principles became action, not merely words.

Yet they began, as most things do, as words. We, my commanders and I, talked to units, to collections of officers, to headquarters, to little groups of men, to individual soldiers casually met as we moved around . . .

General Slim then described the reactions of different nationalities to these addresses.

I learnt, too, that one did not need to be an orator to be effective. Two things were necessary: first to know what you were talking about, and, second and most important, to believe it yourself. I found that if one kept the bulk of one's talk to the material things that men were interested in, food, pay, leave, beer, mails, and the progress of operations, it was safe to end on a higher note—the spiritual foundations—and I always did.

To convince the men in the less spectacular or less obviously important jobs that they were very much part of the army, my commanders and I made it our business to visit these units, to show an interest in them, and to tell them how we and the rest of the army depended upon them. There are in the army, and for that matter any big organization, very large numbers of people whose existence is only remembered when something for which they are responsible goes wrong. Who thinks of the telephone operator until he fails to get his connection, of the cipher officer until he makes a mistake in his decoding, of the orderlies who carry papers about a big headquarters until they take them to the wrong people, of the cook until he makes a particularly foul mess of the interminable bully? Yet they *are* important. It was harder to get this over to the Indian subordinates. They were often drawn from the lower castes, quite illiterate, and used to being looked down upon by their higher-caste fellow-townsmen or villagers. With them, I found I had great success by using the simile of a clock. 'A clock is like an army,' I used to tell them. 'There's a main spring, that's the Army Commander, who makes it all go; then there are other springs, driving the wheels round, those are his generals. The wheels are the officers and men. Some are big wheels, very important, they are the chief staff officers and the colonel sahibs. Other wheels are little ones, that do not look at all important. They are like you. Yet stop one of those little wheels and see what happens to the rest of the clock! They *are* important!'

We played on this very human desire of every man to feel himself and his work important, until one of the most striking things about our army was the way the administrative, labour and non-combatant units acquired a morale which rivalled that of the fighting formations. They felt they shared directly in the triumphs of the Fourteenth Army and that its success and its honour were in their hands as much as anybody's. Another way in which we made every man feel he was part of the show was by keeping him, whatever his rank, as far as was practicable in the picture of what was going on around him. This, of course, was easy with staff officers and similar people by means of conferences held daily or weekly when each branch or department could explain what it had been doing and what it hoped to do. At these conferences they not only discussed

things as a team, but what was equally important, actually
saw themselves as a team. For the men, talks by their officers
and visits to the information centres which were established in
every unit took the place of those conferences.

It was in these ways we laid the spiritual foundations, but
that was not enough; .they would have crumbled without the
others, the intellectual and the material. Here we had first to
ccnvince the doubters that our object, the destruction of the
Japanese Army in battle, was practicable. We had to a great
extent frightened ourselves by our stories of the superman.
Defeated soldiers in their own defence have to protest that
their adversary was something out of the ordinary, that he had
all the advantages of preparation, equipment, and terrain, and
that they themselves suffered from every corresponding handicap. The harder they have run away, the more they must
exaggerate the unfair superiority of the enemy. Thus many
of those who had scrambled out of Burma without waiting to
get to grips with the invader, or who had been in the rear areas
in 1943, had the most hair-raising stories of Japanese super-
efficiency. Those of us who had really fought him, believed that
man for man our soldiers could beat him at his own jungle
game, and that, in intelligence and skill, we could excel and
outwit him.

We were helped, too, by a very cheering piece of news that
now reached us, and of which, as a morale raiser, I made great
use. In August and September 1942, Australian troops had, at
Milne Bay in New Guinea, inflicted on the Japanese their first
undoubted defeat on land . . .

*General Slim also ordered aggressive patrolling in the forward
areas, and larger scale actions designed to build up unit and
formation self-confidence.*

We had laid the first of our intellectual foundations of
morale; everyone knew we could defeat the Japanese; our
object *was* attainable.

The next foundations, that the men should feel that they
belonged to an efficient organization, that the Fourteenth Army
was well run and would get somewhere, followed partly from
these minor successes. At the same time the gradual, but very
noticeable, improvements that General Giffard's re-organiza-
tion of the rear areas and Snelling's and the line of communication staff's almost incredible achievements within the

army itself were making themselves felt. Rations did improve, though still far below what they should be; mail began to arrive more regularly; there were even signs of a welfare service . . .

Other steps towards higher morale included the improvement of rest and training facilities, the reinforcement of disciplinary standards such as saluting, and the institution of a theatre news-paper. When Admiral Mountbatten arrived to take command of the newly-formed South East Asia Command, his presence and personal talks to the troops proved to be a 'final tonic' to morale. Meanwhile supplies or material gradually improved, but due to the priority of the war in Europe they remained small compared to the needs of the Fourteenth Army, a reason which General Slim was careful to explain to the soldiers.

These things were frankly put to the men by their commanders at all levels and, whatever their race, they responded. In my experience it is not so much asking men to fight or work with inadequate or obsolete equipment that lowers morale but the belief that those responsible are accepting such a state of affairs. If men realise that everyone above them and behind them is flat out to get the things required for them, they will do wonders, as my men did, with the meagre resources they have instead of sitting down moaning for better.

I do not say that the men of the Fourteenth Army welcomed difficulties, but they grew to take a fierce pride in overcoming them by determination and ingenuity. From start to finish they had only two items of equipment that were never in short supply : their brains and their courage. They lived up to the unofficial motto I gave them, 'God helps those who help themselves.' Anybody could do an easy job, we told them. It would take real men to overcome the shortages and difficulties we should be up against—the tough chap for the tough job! We had no *corps d'élite* which got preferential treatment; the only units who got that were the ones in front. Often, of course, they went short owing to the difficulties of transportation, but, if we had the stuff and could by hook or crook get it to them they had it in preference to those farther back. One of the most convincing evidences or morale was how those behind— staffs and units—accepted this, and deprived themselves to ensure it. I indulged in a little bit of theatricality in this my-self. When any of the forward formations had to go on half rations, as throughout the campaign they often did, I used to put my headquarters on half rations too. It had little practical effect, but as a gesture it was rather valuable, and it did remind the young staff officers with healthy appetites that it was urgent to get the forward formations back to full rations as soon as possible.

The fair deal meant, too, no distinction between races or castes in treatment. The wants and needs of the Indian, African, and Gurkha soldier had to be looked after as keenly as those of his British comrade. This was not always easy as many of our staff officers, having come straight from home, were, with the best will in the world, ignorant of what these wants were. There were a few, too, who thought that all Indian or African troops required was a bush to lie under and a handful of rice to eat. The Indian soldier's needs are not so numerous or elaborate as the Britisher's, but his morale can be affected just as severely by lack of them.

In another respect we had no favourites. I was frequently asked as the campaign went on, 'Which is your crack division?' I always replied 'All my divisions are crack divisions!' This was true in the sense that at some time or other every division I ever had in the Fourteenth Army achieved some outstanding feat of arms, and it might be any division that at any given period was leading the pack. The men or each division believed that their division was the best in the whole army, and it was right they should, but it is very unwise to let any formation, however good, be publicly recognized as better than the others. The same thing applies to units, and this was especially important where we had fighting together battalions with tremendous names handed down from the past, newly raised ones with their traditions yet to make, men of recognised martial races and others drawn from sources that had up to now no military record. They all got the same treatment and they were all judged by results. Sometimes the results were by no means in accordance with accepted tables of precedence.

The individual, we took pains to ensure, too, was judged on his merits without any undue prejudice in favour of race, caste, or class. This is not always as easy as it sounds or as it ought to be, but I think, promotion, for instance, went by merit whether the officer was British or Indian, Regular or emergency commissioned. In an army of hundreds of thousands many injustices to individuals were bound to occur but, thanks mainly to officers commanding units, most of the Fourteenth Army would, I believe, say that on the whole they had as individuals, a reasonably fair deal. At any rate we did our best to give it to them.

In these and in many other ways we translated my rough notes on the foundations of moral, spiritual, intellectual, and material, into a fighting spirit for our men and a confidence in themselves and their leaders that was to impress our friends and surprise our enemies.

Lord Attlee

Lord Attlee served as Labour Prime Minister of Great Britain from 1945 to 1951. This extract is taken from 'In the Driver's Seat', an article which appeared in The Observer Week-end Review on 18 October 1964. It is printed here not to suggest that Lord Attlee was a better leader than any other prime minister, but because it contains the reflections of a leader on a group composed of other senior leaders. Again the leader's concerns with task, team maintenance and individual needs may be picked out in their distinctive form in this situation, and some of the functions by which they were met. Choosing members of the team is often a key function, and Lord Attlee's remarks upon this matter are full of interest.

In a way it [forming a Cabinet] is more difficult than winning the election, because in choosing his Cabinet the Prime Minister is on his own, and carries the can for his mistakes. Once the appointments have been made, he is going to be stuck with them for a considerable period. If some of the choices soon look unsatisfactory, he cannot start sacking them right away. However, he must give each man a chance, and stand the racket while he improves, grows to the job. If the Prime Minister starts pushing his departmental heads, the morale of the Cabinet as a whole will suffer.

The qualities of the ideal Cabinet Minister are : judgment, strength of character, experience of affairs, and an understanding of ordinary people.

Judgment is necessary because the Cabinet is the instrument by which decisions are reached with a view to action, and decisions stem from judgment. A Cabinet is not a place for eloquence—one reason why good politicians are not always good Cabinet Ministers. It is judgment which is needed to make important decisions on imperfect knowledge in a limited time. Men either have it, or they haven't. They can develop it, if they have it; but cannot acquire it if they haven't.

Strength of character is required to stand up to criticism from other Cabinet members, pressure from outside groups, and the advice of civil servants.

It is also necessary when policies, on which the Cabinet has agreed, are going through the doldrums, or are beginning to fail. A man of character will neither be, nor seem to be, bowed down by this. Nor will he be blown about by 'every wind of vain doctrine'.

Lord Attlee then discussed the value of a wide general experience in cabinet members.

It is more important that the Cabinet discussion should take place, so to speak, at a higher level than the information and opinions provided by the various departmental briefs. A collection of departmental Ministers does not make a Cabinet. A Cabinet consists only of responsible human beings. And it is their thinking and judgment in broad terms that make a Government tick, not arguments about the recommendations of civil servants. It is interesting to note that quite soon a Cabinet begins to develop a group personality. The rôle of the Prime Minister is to cultivate this, if it is efficient and right-minded; to do his best to modify it, if it is not.

While a collection of departmental heads mouthing their top civil servants' briefs is unsatisfactory, a collection of Ministers who are out of touch with administration tends to be unrealistic. And a Minister who has an itch to run everybody else's department as well as, or in preference to his own, is just a nuisance. Some men will be ready to express a view about everything. They should be discouraged. If necessary, I would shut them up. Once is enough. Ernie Bevin held forth on a variety of subjects, but Ernie had an extraordinary variety of practical knowledge.

It is a curious thing that nearly every Cabinet throws up at least one man, whether he is a departmental Minister or not, of whom a newcomer might ask, 'What is *he* doing here?' He is there because he is wise. You will hear a junior Cabinet Minister being told by the Prime Minister, perhaps, 'If you are going to do that, old boy, you would be well advised to have a talk with X.'

The ability to talk attractively in Cabinet is not essential. Being able to put a case clearly and succinctly and simply is what counts. The Cabinet is certainly not the place for rhetoric. Though an excellent head of department and a conciliator of genius, Nye Bevan used to talk a bit too much occasionally. Usually he was extremely good, often wise, and sometimes extremely wise; '75 per cent of political wisdom is a sense of priorities,' I remember him saying once—an admirable remark, and good advice for Cabinet Ministers.

The occasions when he talked too much were when he got excited because he felt that our policies were falling short of the pure milk of the word. This goes for most such interruptions, and a Prime Minister should try to avoid these time-consuming expressions of guilt—or electoral fear—by trying to reassure from time to time the pure in heart who feel the Government is backsliding.

However, you cannot choose people according to what makes an ideal Cabinet Minister. In the first place, you must choose people with regard to keeping balance within the party. This need not be overdone. It is a matter of democratic common-sense, not a craven below-the-scenes manipulation. It would not do to have all trade unionists in a Labour Cabinet, or all constituency members, or all middle-class intellectuals, or all ornaments of the Co-operative Party. Some working-class trade unionists are in fact honorary members of the intelligentsia—Nye again—while I have known upper-class intellectuals try desperately to behave like heavy-handed sons of toil . . .

A Prime Minister must have his own view of a man's capacity to serve in the Cabinet. Nor can selected members always have the job they want. High qualifications are required for the most important posts in the Cabinet.

The Cabinet usually meets once a week. That should be enough for regular meetings, and should be if they grasp from the start what they are there for. They should be back at their work as soon as possible, and a Prime Minister should put as little as possible in their way. We started sharp at 11, and rose in time for lunch. Even in a crisis, another couple of meetings should be enough in the same week : if there is a crisis, the less talk the better.

The Prime Minister shouldn't speak too much himself in Cabinet. He should start the show or ask somebody else to do so, and then intervene only to bring out the more modest chaps who, despite their seniority, might say nothing if not asked. And the Prime Minister must sum up. Experienced Labour leaders should be pretty good at this; they have spent years attending debates at meetings of the Parliamentary Party and the National Executive, and have to sum *those* up. That takes some doing – good training for the Cabinet.

Particularly when a non-Cabinet Minister is asked to attend, especially if it is his first time, the Prime Minister may have to be cruel. The visitor may want to show how good he is, and go on too long. A good thing is to take no chance and ask him to send the Cabinet a paper in advance. The Prime Minister can then say, 'A very clear statement, Minister of—. Do you need to add anything?' in a firm tone of voice obviously expecting the answer, *No*. If somebody else looks like making a speech, it is sound to nip in with 'Has anybody any objection?' If somebody starts to ramble, a quick, 'Are you *objecting*? You're not? Right. Next business,' and the Cabinet can move on.

It is essential for the Cabinet to move on, leaving in its wake a trail of clear, crisp, uncompromising decisions. This is what government is about. And the challenge to democracy is how to get it done quickly.

An Unknown Worker

This description of leadership on the shop floor is taken from J. A. C. Brown's book 'The Social Psychology of Industry', pages 83 and 84.

Briefly, it was found that absenteeism and high labour turnover occurred predominantly amongst those workers who did not make a team, who had not managed to fit into any group (either because of personal peculiarities or, more usually, because they had not been given the opportunity to do so).

Having no social background, they had no feelings of loyalty and took little interest in what went on around them in the factory. On the other hand, investigation of a work team which had a production record 25 per cent above the average for the firm, showed up some of the factors which lead to good morale in the workshop. This group of men was recognized by the other workers as being somewhat clannish in that its members felt themselves to be superior to other groups—that is to say, they showed loyalty and pride of membership. The foreman of the department where the group was employed was a busy man and rarely visited it, while his senior assistant visited it only once a day. All the work was in charge of a man who had no official standing whatever, but was the natural leader of the team. This man had both the time (in that he was not distracted by the necessity of dealing with technical problems) and the ability to concentrate on group solidarity. He handled this problem in the following manner : all new employees were introduced to the other members of the team and placed with those who seemed likely to make congenial associates; later, they were taken to the end of the assembly line to see where the part being made in the department fitted into the finished article. All complaints were dealt with at once by the leader, but if they were beyond his powers to handle he referred them to higher authority. The individual workers were in these ways given significance (they saw how their job fitted into the whole), comradeship (in being members of a team), and an awareness of being fairly treated.

R.S.M. John Lord

Brought up a Grenadier Guardsman, Mr Lord became a Company Sergeant Major at Sandhurst and then R.S.M. of the 3rd Battalion of The Parachute Regiment at its birth in October 1941. Captured at Arnhem he was incarcerated along with about 2,000 others from the British 1st Airborne Division in Stalag XI B. Gradually, hut by hut, his leadership spread until he finally gained control of the entire camp of 17,000 prisoners of all nationalities. These extracts are from a tape-recording made by Mr Lord for the author in 1966.

41

Eventually we moved into the huts which had been occupied by the Poles from Warsaw. It was a much better compound. There were, I think, six huts planned to hold about 200 men each in this one compound, and there was an open space which we could use as a football field nearby. At the same time as numbers grew each hut had to hold about 450 men, the winter was very severe, food was extremely short . . . There were no cleaning materials, the huts tended to get into a terrible state, but we managed to get some twigs from working parties that went out to get wood, and so we would keep the floors swept.

I insisted, gradually, that every man made his bed properly with his one blanket, and that the bed space was his responsibility and was clean, and his little box in which he kept his precious articles was tidy, and that all the rooms were swept out. And I also insisted, this was very important too, although it caused a lot of grumbles at times, that all the windows were opened in the morning and that every man jack who could walk at all went out for exercise round the compound in the morning. This was vital to their health. I was greatly assisted in this by the encouragement of the British doctors with whom I worked closely, and who did a wonderful job under most difficult circumstances.

Here I would like to say how interesting it was to see the individual behaviour of the men, and this deeply applied as time wore on and men from other units started coming in. You could pick out men who came from what I would call good battalions, well disciplined, happy battalions. They tended, almost straight away, to start to look after themselves, to keep themselves clean and as decent as possible and to muck in. To the other men—now of course these are generalisations, I know, but I think that they are true—who probably came from not quite such a good unit, the opposite applied in so many cases.

All this caused a lot of comment among the senior members of my team. Because, having mentioned that we had moved into this large compound, this gave me an opportunity to start some sort of military organisation going under our own steam. I built a set-up with each hut rather like a company, and when the time came for the majority of warrant and non-commissioned officers to go to a more suitable camp for them, I had had time to get to know a lot of them much better. I knew some of my own men, of course. I went round having hand picked six or seven senior leaders I wanted, all WOs whom I judged would be the ones to carry out the task ahead of us, and I am very glad and proud to say that every man I approached without fail volunteered to stay with me, although he had every right to think that had he moved on to another camp, a British camp, the conditions would have been much better for him. Everyone stayed, and what a magnificent job they did. We set up this military organisation, rather similar to the one to which the men were accustomed, and in addition I sent one of my own Company Sergeant Majors from the Battalion up to the Hospital to do the administration there. He did a magnificent job. So that was a start.

Mr Lord then established his right to take the first part of the morning Roll Call parade before handing it over to the Germans. This meant that British soldiers heard words of command from their own Warrant Officer. To make sure that every man knew what Mr Lord's aims were he set up informal briefing groups in every hut. Meanwhile he made certain that his own personal turnout was as smart as possible in the circumstances. Daily bugle calls sounded on an old Belgian trumpet by a British prisoner served not only to maintain morale but also to impress the other nationalities, as did the simple military honours insisted upon by Mr Lord at the frequent funerals. Concerts and soccer matches also enhanced morale when the Germans would allow them. Most important of all, food rations, Red Cross parcels and firewood had to be seen to be justly distributed. In this situation the leader had to be ruthless in putting the group interest before that of any particular individual.

One of the worst offences one can commit in circumstances such as these is to steal another man's ration. Now several cases of this occurred and it was extremely difficult to detect and to prove. However, one day one of the CSMs came to me and told me he was quite convinced that a certain man, who had come into the camp recently, was responsible for one of these thefts. On the information I received I interviewed this man and questioned him for a couple of hours or more in the evening by the light of a small lamp, questioning and questioning until eventually this little man broke down and admitted that he had stolen this ration.

So here was a self-confessed thief, a very serious problem which could lead to the most terrible consequences of fighting and distrust and so on in the camp. What was I going to do about it? I never had any powers of punishment in those circumstances. I could tell him he would be court-martialled after the war, but what was the good of that? They couldn't care less. It had to be done by leadership and example. So, rightly or wrongly, I decided to take a drastic step. I ordered him to report to me next morning.

I went out on the morning roll call at 7 o'clock in the first light and I made him stand behind me. Having called the parade to attention, and stood the men easy, I got them all to look in my direction and produced this little man, and said, 'Here you are, mark him well, this man is a thief'. I briefly and without elaboration told them what had happened. Now, some people nowadays would say, 'What a dreadful thing to brand a man like that'. But which is more important, the interests of the men as a whole, or this individual? I was very worried in myself afterwards whether or not I had gone too far, but I am quite sure I hadn't, because I don't think we had one more case of thieving after that. And, of course, it may have prevented a tremendous lot more thieving, and, what is worse, violence.

With the New Year of 1945 allied prisoners began to arrive in Stalag XI B, some captured during the initially successful German offensive in the Ardennes, and some from Poland, now threatened by the Russians.

It is of these men that I want to speak now because I had this responsibility completely upon my shoulders alone. The first lot who came in, after the New Year of course, were in good shape, they had come by train ... The next sight to greet my eyes was the first arrival of those who had had to march on foot for all those hundreds and hundreds of miles. I really never would have believed it possible. I saw some of them in the hospital, and saw those who succumbed, and I later saw the photographs of Belsen camp, and I can assure everybody that many of these men were in exactly the same state as those victims of Belsen. They were put into the huge marquees with only straw on the ground. Major Smith and his doctors went down. He came back and said, 'Mr Lord, I have segregated 300 of these men, and if these 300 do not receive, immediately, more food, and are not moved into better accommodation, they will die'. He was quite adamant about this.

What was I to do? First of all I put the word round our men what the position was. I shall never forget it. They quite voluntarily offered, each man, to give up a little, a very little, of their own food for these 300 men. Secondly, I went down to the first lot of British prisoners who had come by train, that I have just mentioned, in the good accommodation and I put the case to them. And 300 of the fittest came forward and volunteered to move out into the marquees, and remember it was jolly cold and it was very uncomfortable, but they volunteered without any pressure from me, after I had spoken to them collectively. These 300 men would at least have got more food and we could have managed a little bit of Red Cross stuff for them, and they would have moved into better accommodation. And this meant that, probably, the majority of those lives would be saved. So here we were. I went to the German Commandant and stated the case to him, quite simply, without embellishments. And to my horror he refused to allow the transfer. This was absolutely incredible and fantastic. I pressed the case; he lost his temper; I went away; and I must have gone up three more times to see him, so worried was I about this serious situation. But he would not allow the move.

I went down to the other two compounds, the one with the marquees with the very, very sick men in, and the one with the volunteers who had offered to change over the accommodation. And I moved the fit men from their compound to the marquees without German permission. I had to do it. I was taking an awful chance, but what was this chance compared with the chance of saving some 300 men?

Of course the repercussions on the German Commandant's side were violent, absolutely violent. But I don't want to go into that. We succeeded, and the majority of those men came home fit, or reasonably fit and well. We lost, I suppose, of that 300 men about one tenth, about 30. So something was achieved. It was known, not only to my men, the actions that I had taken but also to every single man in that prison camp.

As time went on, it bore more and more upon me, particularly as it was obvious that the British and American armies were going to advance as the weather improved, what was going to

45

happen in the camp when the time came, when the war, possibly suddenly, collapsed or came to an end? It could quite possibly do so before we were reached by our own allies. What was going to happen in the camp? What were the plans? There were several possibilities. One grave possibility was this. Opposite the camp, across the road were magnificent barracks in which were housed the SS Panzer Grenadiers, young Hitler fanatics. Now supposed Germany suddenly capitulated, what would the reactions of these young men be? Would they remember Hitler's words of dragging Europe down in flames with the Reich? This was not the realms of fancy; this was a distinct possibility and was not only my thought alone. It was the thought throughout the camp. Would they turn their weapons against the prisoners in this prison camp, all these different nationalities, in revenge and exterminate them? But what had been done about it? I could find out nothing. There had been no liaison between nationalities; I asked questions round about and literally nothing had been done. What were we going to do? Were we just going to sit there and hope for the best? This did not seem to me to be good enough. But who was going to do it? And how were we going to set about it? Well I was spoken to, talked to, by great friends of mine, Bill Kibble, Don Rice and others, and they impressed upon me, although I suppose secretly in myself I realised this, that I must be the man to get things organised. So I asked Sgt.-Major Wickham, who knew so many of these other nationalities and whose great asset was that he knew who could be trusted. If we were going to lay plans for our actions when the camp was liberated or when the war finished, if that happened before, then those in our confidence must be absolutely reliable men. There must be no chance of one whisper, because if one whisper had got to the ears of the German authorities Heaven knows what their punishment of us would have been.

Sam Wickham sought out a representative from each of the nationalities whom he believed could be trusted. Let's see, there was the Frenchman (we knew we had a good representative there), a Russian, a Serbian doctor, a Belgian, a Dutchman and one or two others in the Committee. We didn't have on the Committee a member of the Polish community and I shouldn't like to be misunderstood about this, because I knew nothing about the Poles at all; I merely acted on the advice

I'd received. But it should be realised how extremely dangerous this was.

So that was the Committee formed. Previous to this, I had had made a map of the camp in which every sentry post was plotted and everything from a security point of view I had worked out. So I set down on paper what I considered should be done . . .

Mr Lord's careful preparations received an unexpected boost when the Commandant asked him to provide unarmed sentries to assist the Germans in keeping order in such matters as food distribution. Five days before the first British tanks arrived Mr Lord and his staff were in virtual control of the 17,000 men in the camp.

All the administration, the feeding and so on we controlled. From the warehouses opposite at the SS Barracks we brought out the food and the clothing, and we shared it out among the members of all nationalities of that camp. And there was no trouble at all that could not be controlled. These were very, very busy days. Five days.

In fact it was on the 16th April, early on, that the news had improved of the advance of the British Army. I received news very early that the British Army were just down the road. I went to the front gate, everything laid on, our sentries there, all nations in their own compounds under control of their own excellent men; in other words everything was in order. I waited. And up the road came a British tank. In the forelager our men were on duty, and the barbed wire inside the forelager was thronged with all these other nationalities. I shall never forget this tank arriving at the front gate with some others behind. The first figure out of that tank, begrimed and dusty, was a corporal of the 8th Hussars, old friends of my days in Egypt, and I was delighted. That corporal, having travelled, fought and campaigned and rushed through in the later stages, jumped out of his tank, spotted me at the gate, and he came up and he stood to attention to report himself. Now this was a wonderful thing for these other nationalities to see, this action by a begrimed corporal . . . When these tanks arrived, we disarmed the German sentries who willingly gave up their arms, and our men took them over. That was the first thing. I took it upon myself to lower the swastika of the Reich and in its place to hoist up our own home-made Union Jack, which had been placed on the coffins of so many funerals. As I raised it and looked up the flagstaff towards the blue heavens I cannot describe my feelings, they were feelings of thankfulness and re-lief, and I hope I am not misunderstood if in myself I gave thanks to God for this moment . . .

Thus with all the possibilities of what might have happened, of internal strife through the liquor which was obviously being brought into the camp, and a thousand and one things, we remained in control and until the day I left, of those 17,000 odd men of so many different nationalities and characters, not one man was injured by any offensive action, and not one man was killed. And when I look back on it I think, 'My word! how different it could have been'. And therefore we had cause to be thankful that things had worked out so well for our well-being in the long run.

Field Marshal Lord Montgomery

Lieut. General Sir Brian Horrocks commanded 13 Corps under Field Marshal Lord Montgomery (as he later became) at the battles of Alam Halfa and Alamein. These passages from his autobiography 'A Full Life' described the impact of Lord Montgomery's leadership upon both himself and the Eighth Army. The first extract illustrates the way a senior leader met both the task and individual needs by developing the professional ability of a subordinate.

On the day after the battle [Alam Halfa] I was sitting in my headquarters purring with satisfaction. The battle had been won and I had not been mauled in the process. What could be better? Then in came a liaison officer from 8th Army head-quarters bringing me a letter in Monty's even hand. This is what he said :

'Dear Jorrocks,

Well done – but you must remember that you are now a corps commander and not a divisional commander . . .'

He went on to list four or five things which I had done wrong, mainly because I had interfered too much with the tasks of my subordinate commanders. The purring stopped abruptly.

Perhaps I wasn't quite such a heaven-sent general after all. But the more I thought over the battle, the more I realised that Monty was right. So I rang him up and said, 'Thank you very much.'

I mention this because Montgomery was one of the few commanders who tried to train the people who worked under him. Who else, on the day after his first major victory, which had altered the whole complexion of the war in the Middle East, would have taken the trouble to write a letter like this in his own hand to one of his subordinate commanders?

The psychological effect of this victory was terrific, for nothing succeeds like success, particularly in war. Troops will always follow a successful general. Monty had unquestionably won the first round in his contest with the Desert Fox; what is more, he had won it in exactly the manner in which he had said beforehand he would win it. Everyone felt that new dynamic force had entered into the tired, rather stale old body of the 8th Army. I, of course, also benefited from the change of heart, and from now on things became much easier.

In Tripoli, after the successful 'break through' at Alamein, Horrocks witnessed an example of the army's affection for its commander—a standing ovation by all ranks before and after a concert-party's performance.

And here in the 8th Army was the same outward and visible sign of the greatest battle-winning factor of all—a spirit of complete trust, confidence and affection within a formation. This sort of happy family atmosphere is common enough in divisions which have lived, trained and grown up together, but it is comparatively rare in higher formations. I know of only two in our army where it existed strongly during the last war— Montgomery's 8th Army and Slim's 14th Army. And it is significant that both men took over their commands at a time when things were going badly and morale was low.

Monty had the harder passage of the two to start with. As we know, the old desert sweats did not welcome him with open arms—far from it. Yet only a few months later, here in Tripoli was this remarkable demonstration of personal affection.

How had it been done? Cynics will say that Montgomery was successful, and that soldiers will always follow a general who wins battles. Wellington's troops never loved him, yet they would have followed him anywhere. I would say that there were four main qualities of leadership which bound the 8th Army to Monty.

First. When all was confusion he had the supreme gift of reducing the most complex situation to simplicity. More than any other man I have ever met he was able to sit back and *think*, with the result that he was never deluded by 'the trees'.

Second. He took infinite pains to explain to every man in the Army exactly what was required of him.

Third. He was very tough mentally, both towards the enemy and, perhaps more important still, towards the political dictation from the United Kingdom. No amount of urging would ever induce him to launch his army into battle before it was ready.

Finally. He was obviously a complete master of his craft, the craft of war.

T. E. Lawrence

Field Marshal Viscount Allenby gave his fullest assessment of T. E. Lawrence in a broadcast which 'The Times' reported on 20 May 1935. Despite criticism of the 'Lawrence legend', his leadership has never been doubted, a fact attested by Lord Allenby— no mean judge.

When first I met him, in the summer of 1917, he had just returned from a venturesome raid behind the Turkish front... Lawrence was under my command, but, after acquainting him with my strategical plan, I gave him a free hand. His co-operation was marked by the utmost loyalty, and I never had anything but praise for his work, which, indeed, was invaluable throughout the campaign.

He was the mainspring of the Arab movement. He knew their language, their manners, their mentality; he understood and shared their merry, sly humour; in daring he led them, in endurance he equalled, if not surpassed, their strongest. Though in complete sympathy with his companions, and sharing to the full with them hardship and danger, he was careful to maintain the dignity of his position as Confidential Adviser to the Emir Feisal. Himself an Emir, he wore the robes of that rank, and kept up a suitable degree of state. His own bodyguard, men of wild and adventurous spirit, were all picked by Lawrence personally. Mounted on thoroughbred camels, they followed him in all his daring rides; and among those reckless desert rangers there was none who would not have willingly died for their chief. In fact, not a few lost their lives through devotion to him and in defence of his person. The shy and retiring scholar—archaeologist-philosopher was swept by the tide of war into a position undreamt of ... and there shone forth a brilliant tactician, with a genius for leadership. Such men win friends—such also find critics and detractors. But the highest reward for success is the inward knowledge that it has been rightly won. Praise or blame was rewarded with indifference by Lawrence. He did his duty as he saw it before him. He has left to us who knew and admired him, a beloved memory.

Lieut. Colonel W. F. Stirling served with T. E. Lawrence in the desert, and recorded his impression of him as a leader in 'T. E. Lawrence By His Friends'.

Lawrence not only saw the task more clearly than others and how it could be achieved, but also possessed a remarkable intuitive sense of what was happening in the minds of the group. Above all he led by example. It was my great good fortune to be appointed General Staff Officer to the Arab group. Above all he led by example. It was my great good final phase of the Arab revolt on till the capture of Damascus, I worked, travelled, and fought alongside Lawrence. Night after night we lay wrapped in our blankets under the cold stars of the desert.

At these times one learns much of a man. Lawrence took the limelight from those of us professional soldiers who were fortunate enough to serve with him, but never once have I heard even a whisper of jealousy. We sensed that we were serving with a man immeasurably our superior.

As I see it, his outstanding characteristic was his clarity of vision and his power of shedding all unessentials from his thoughts, added to his uncanny knowledge of what the other man was thinking and doing.

Think of it! A young second lieutenant of the Egyptian Expeditionary Force goes down the Arabian coast to where a sporadic revolt of the Western Arabs had broken out against their Turkish masters. Then, with the help of a few British officers, all senior to himself, and professional soldiers, who willingly placed themselves under his general guidance, he galvanizes the Arab revolt into a coherent whole. By his daring courage, his strategy, his novel tactics, he welds the turbulent Arab tribes into a fighting machine of such value that he is able to immobilize two Turkish divisions and provide a flank force for Lord Allenby's final advance through Palestine and Syria, the value of which that great general acknowledged again and again.

No one, looking at Lawrence, would have considered him strong physically. The fact remains that this man was to break all the records of Arabia for speed and endurance. The great sagas sung throughout the desert of phenomenal rides carried out by dispatch riders and dating back to the days of Caliph Haroun Al-Raschid have been completely eclipsed by Lawrence's achievements. On one occasion he averaged 100 miles a day for three consecutive days. Such endurance as this is almost incredible. I myself have ridden 50 miles in a night, but never do I want to do it again. The difficulty is to keep awake. After the bitter glow of the desert night when the sun begins to rise and a warm glow envelops everything, the urge to sleep becomes a veritable torture. If you sleep you are apt to fall, and it is a long way from the top of a camel to the ground.

What was it that enabled Lawrence to seize and hold the imagination of the Arabs? It is a difficult question to answer. The Arabs were noted individualists, intractable to a degree, and without any sense of discipline. Yet it was sufficient for almost any one of us to say that Lawrence wanted something done, and forthwith it was done.

How did he gain this power? The answer may partly be that he represented the heart of the Arab movement for freedom, and the Arabs realized that he had vitalized their cause; that he could do everything and endure everything just a little better than the Arabs themselves; that by his investment with the gold dagger of Mecca he ranked with the Ashraf or the descendants of the Prophet, and the Emir Feisal treated him as a brother and an equal.

But chiefly, I think, we must look for the answer in Lawrence's uncanny ability to sense the feelings of any group

52

of men in whose company he found himself; his power to probe behind their minds and to uncover the well-springs of their actions.

Lord Hunt

Lord Hunt led the first successful assault on Mount Everest in 1953. His views are drawn from 'The Top' in the Observer Weekend Review of 21 June 1965. This article took the form of a reported interview between Lord Hunt and Kenneth Harris.

Climbing with companions creates a wonderfully close relationship, of co-operation and sharing, which is rarely found in everyday life. To tackle a hard climb is a test of each individual's intellect, experience, will, guts and skill. But each is dependent on the other; not only for achievement, but for mutual security and survival.

This is the quintessence of team-work, in which each is playing an equal part, and all have complete confidence in one another. It is the very opposite of the gang idea ...

Other people come into your mountain picture both because you all enjoy doing it—because you are kindred spirits—and because with rare exceptions a man cannot safely and successfully achieve a big climb 'solo'.

On short rock-climbs it is somewhat different, but the principle and the spirit of the thing is, or should be, the same. I personally don't care for the competitive spirit which has crept in, with the increasing numbers of ever-rising standards of technical performance of our younger climbers. In the Soviet Union climbing is organised on a competitive basis even for the biggest mountains.

I have never seen mountaineering like that. The contest in mountaineering is between you and the mountain : or, better, between two sides within yourself. Not between you and your fellow men. Other human beings come into the relationship not as competitors, but as collaborators.

Lord Hunt was then asked if there was any 'fundamental difference' between tackling a mountain in Cumberland or Derbyshire and climbing Everest. Besides the physical contrasts

53

Lord Hunt mentioned the psychological stress encountered at high altitudes.

The combined effect of the rarefied atmosphere, prolonged risk and discomfort, make people edgy and awkward. You're inclined to be intolerant, to see things out of proportion. You can become very selfish—get peevish if you don't think you have had your fair share of the food; get a 'fixture' about someone else's personal habits—things which you would laugh at anybody for noticing, let alone resenting, in normal conditions.

I would like to make another point about speed in climbing : it is a tremendously important aspect of safety. On a short rock climb in this country you can afford to be slow and careful in climbing a route on a cliff of 500–600 feet in height; there is time to take every possible precaution. In the Alps, you must learn to move faster, even on difficult ground, or you will be benighted. You may plan to do so, but the longer you are on a climb, under tension, with the ever-present chance of bad weather setting in, the greater the risk.

On a Himalayan climb you are physically slowed down and the climb becomes more like a siege : advancing with your shelter, food and equipment slowly upwards by stages. So the climb takes a long time and the chances are much smaller on this account. Hence the need for oxygen, to reduce the risks, increase the pace and thus the chance of success.

Physiological wastage and deterioration are very marked in a man at 25,000 feet and above. The sheer effort of getting out of a sleeping bag, of putting on boots, of cooking, require an immense effort of will—let alone the climbing.

Harris 'I'm interested in this point about will power, Is it just that you need more of it, the higher you go ?'

Yes, for all the reasons I've mentioned. But to get to the top of the highest mountains you need to apply your will power to the achievement well in advance—not merely when you are there. In a sense you have to do the climb in your mind before you start. This is because of the many circumstances which combine to reduce your powers of determination at the time, and which limit your ability to think clearly. Predetermination is a most important aspect of a successful Himalayan climb.

*   *   *

Harris 'You mentioned exposure. Do you mean getting cold?'

No; not just that. Exposure on mountains has two distinct meanings. There is the sense of being out on a vast precipice, on small holds or on steep ice, with space beneath your feet and the nearest level ground several hundreds or thousands of feet below you. That's one meaning of exposure.

Then there is the physiological sense, of prolonged exposure to the elements, not only to cold, but even more to damp and wind and the exposure of the mind to loneliness and fear. This kind of exposure is the combination of physical strain and psychological anxiety; it varies with the degree of risk and the time you continue to run it.

Common to both types of exposure, I believe, is fear. And the answer to both aspects of exposure is training—or experience —and good technique. Knowing what you should be doing in any predicament. It not only increases your chances of survival and focuses your faculties on what you are doing; it also exorcises the hypnotic spell which the sense of exposure casts about you. A number of accidents in our own hills are due to exposure, due to lack of experience.

Harris 'Is mountaineering really all about the facing of fear?'

No. The facing of fear is involved, inevitably. But that isn't the only motive. Most men who climb mountains don't do so because they are driven by a neurotic obsession with the need to face their own fears. Though, as I said to you earlier on, they find they have to do so, time and again, in the process of climbing mountains. But as I also said, a very powerful motive is the comradeship which comes from sharing a risk, which reduces your fears.

I would say another one is the exercise of judgment in the face of danger—the opposite of foolhardiness. It may require more moral courage to abandon a climb than to go on. It is the fanatic, or the addict who lives on fear like a drug, who insists on going on, sometimes to his death. Most men who climb mountains do so because they enjoy it and because they want to go on doing so.

Some years ago in the Caucasus, near the summit of a 17,000-foot peak and with most of the technical difficulties behind and below us, a climbing party of which I was a member decided that the objective dangers of continuing to the top were such that we should turn back—only 600 feet below our much-desired goal. It was a hard decision, but this happens frequently to every mountaineer.

We went back to base. Our Russian friends were amazed that we had turned back and, I think, because we freely admitted it. For me, accepting that a situation is too big for me, and deliberately acting on that decision to bow to it, is moral victory. It is the open-eyed acceptance of one's circumstances and shortcomings which is the essence of humility. And humility is one of the ingredients of leadership.

This brings me back to your first question : Why do men climb mountains? It is just as well to answer it, for yourself, sooner rather than later, because the wrong reasons can lead to the wrong decisions at moments of crisis.

You see, Kenneth, to my mind it is not getting to the top of Everest that matters in life—it is why and how you try to get there. And sometimes it is better not to get to the top of a mountain at all. The victor on a mountain is the man who can conquer his own ambitions if need be.

CHAPTER THREE

LEADERSHIP SELECTION

The last chapter gave the reader an opportunity to look at concrete examples which illustrate one or more of the aspects of
leadership discussed in Chapter 1. It is hoped that these 'case-
studies' will have put some flesh-and-blood on what otherwise
might have remained a skeleton of theory : a delight to the
anatomist but to no one else. In this chapter, which is largely
historical, the first major experiment in applying the functional
approach to leadership on a large scale will be recounted. The
successful results of that experiment should also serve to remind us
throughout the rest of the book that in considering the functional
approach we are no longer dealing with an unproven theory on
the nature of leadership, but one that has been imaginatively
tried and tested for over a quarter of a century.

In May 1942 a group of psychologists and psychiatrists who
had individually been 'called up' into the British Army for the
duration of the Second World War, came together to devise a new
method of officer selection. The old approach whereby the candidate for a commission was interviewed by a committee of senior
officers intent on spotting his leadership 'qualities' had turned
out to be ineffective : a large number of cadets selected in this
way had had to be subsequently returned to their units as unfit for
promotion. In place of these interviews the team devised a series
of three-day conferences which became known as War Office
Selection Boards (popularly known as 'Wosbies' from their initials,
W.O.S.B.) from 1942. Fortunately one of this pioneering team,
Dr Henry Harris, who himself served on the staff of a number of
the early conferences attended by some 6,000 potential officers,

has left us in his *The Group Approach to Leadership Testing,* an invaluable 'individual reaction to a collective effort', from which the subsequent quotations are taken.[1]

Before considering the W.O.S.B. method in detail, it is both interesting and worthwhile to note how the Army as a whole came to be persuaded to embrace the new approach. In his foreword to Dr Harris' book General Sir Ronald Adam, who was Adjutant General of the Forces 1941–46, gave a short account of this important piece of reform :

> The Army, during the early days of the war, carried out its selection of candidates for training as officers by interview boards. It was clear that these were not being successful. The failure rate at O.C.T.U.s [Officer Cadet Training Units] was high, and I know one course at an O.C.T.U. when 50 per cent of the course failed to pass out. This was a waste of time and had unfortunate effects even on good candidates, for the knowledge of a high failure rate did not give confidence to those attending.
>
> The interview had a deterrent effect on potential officers too. The average candidate did not feel that he was being given a fair chance, and there was a completely mistaken impression that the questions asked favoured the public school boy at the expense of those not so educated.
>
> The decision to change the old methods was taken after a trial board, when groups of presidents interviewed candidates and recorded their opinions separately. This showed so marked a difference of the opinions expressed on the same candidate that a new method had to be found.
>
> Early experiments were based on the test which the German Army had employed from 1923 onwards, apparently to their satisfaction, but these were not a success.
>
> The experimental board, which tested its methods by judging the officers attending a Company Commanders' School, produced a system that showed promising results, and these were continually improved until the system described by the author evolved.
>
> The first board set up under the new system proved that the candidate considered that it was a great improvement on the old interview. In the Command in which it worked the number of volunteers for commissions went up by 25 per cent. It is to

be remembered that no one could be forced to take a commission.

Great efforts were made to validate results, but the Army was working against time in producing the continual stream of officers required by units, and validation could not be complete. To my mind the best validation was that the candidates going before the boards were satisfied that they had been given a fair chance to show their mettle and there was no discrimination or favouritism.

In these sentences we may see the sequence of reform in any organisation. It may be summarised as follows :

1. A widespread feeling that present methods are inadequate. The reformer must convert this feeling into conviction by producing some concrete evidence to support it.
2. A period of 'trial and error' experimentation. (This may overlap with 1.)
3. The production and trial running of a possible new method. A comparison of it with the old methods by some form of evaluation.
4. A general introduction of the new method, and a confirmation of its value. (In the case of W.O.S.B. note the importance of the candidate's reactions as one of the criteria for assessing the relative merits of the methods.)

Having briefly mentioned the then recent work of Kurt Lewin and others on the 'dynamics of inter personal relationships' Dr Harris moved to a description of the theories upon which the W.O.S.B. method of selection was based. Although his background as a psychotherapist who had come to selection *via* group-psychotherapy conditioned the author's discussion of the small group (as he readily admits) it is clear that the research team behind W.O.S.B. had seized upon the key ideas of the situational and functional approaches, as described above in Chapter 1. It was understood, for example, that groups with different 'characteristic working situations' might require dissimilar leaders. In particular, small military groups which would have to operate in the stress conditions of the battlefield needed a leader who could function efficiently under stress. The essential problem was how to select the right man for the right group :

W.O.S.B's answer was to test and evaluate him in the context of the small experimental group submitted to considerable time and problem stress, i.e. required to execute a difficult task against time.

That which one sought to observe and evaluate one might call his group-effectiveness, the sum total of his contribution to the group and its task. In this book we will differentiate group-effectiveness into the following components:

1. the effective *level of his functioning*: of his ability to contribute towards the functional aspect of the common task by planning and organising the available abilities, materials, time, etc.
2. his *group-cohesiveness* or ability to bind the group in the direction of the common task: to relate its members emotionally to each other and to the task.
3. his *stability* or ability to stand up to resistance and frustrations without serious impairment of (1) or (2) and the results of their interplay. [*Cf. 'Stability' is not a very dynamic term for what is essentially a dynamic concept, i.e. the active and continuous capacity not only to resist the deteriorating effects of stress, but also to return to normal when these have passed off . . . Mental stamina might do (as a better word) (p. 33).*]

In short, in the W.O.S.B. technique of officer selection, one observes a man *in* a group-task in order to determine his group-effectiveness (in a particular field): one selects and *tests* him *in* a group *for* a group.

Although emphasising that it was too early to attempt a definitive formulation on the nature of leadership Dr Harris tentatively suggested that the whole of it may be represented by the concept of 'group-effectiveness' as analysed above. Both 'general factors' (those which determine a man's level of general leadership in a group, regardless of task) and 'specific factors' (those which equip him to lead in relation to certain tasks) could be described as 'group-effectiveness'. As Dr Harris wrote in a thoughtful summary:

One may suggest provisionally that leadership is the measure and degree of an individual's ability to influence—and be influenced by—a group in the implementation of a common task. This circumscribes three important aspects of leadership function: the individual, the group and the task: and indicates leadership as a functional relationship between these three basic variables.

In respect of the first two, it can only be highly effective if based on a sensitive understanding of the group's needs and on the ability to be influenced by it. The leader who dominates and drives a group towards an end they do not seek is unlikely to retain his leadership : his domination is brittle and will stand little stress. In so far as he considers the needs and mobilises the initiative of every member in the group; in so far as he helps them towards the goal which will give the group its greatest satisfaction and provide every member of it with the profound gratification of effective participation on his own level, and at his own optimum tempo . . . his leadership is more real, more flexible, more resistant to stress, and incidentally more democratic—in the best sense of the word—than any leadership which is insensitive to the group in which it is exercised. (p. 19)

The 'Leaderless Group' or 'Stress Group Task' formed the most characteristic and long-enduring technique of selection employed by W.O.S.B. In essence the idea was simple : eight candidates in an experimental 'micro-community' were given a series of tasks to perform while one or more observers stood by to spot and record the task and team maintenance (or group-cohesive) functions which each member naturally performed. The tasks varied in character (e.g. outdoor physical, indoor planning, and group-discussion), and also in the amount of stress latent in each situation, but the size and composition of the group remained the same. It appeared to be unorganised (with no appointed leaders) but as regards its task it could be directed or undirected :

In the W.O.S.B. Group Discussion—an indoor task involving the management of men and ideas—the discussion is usually undirected, i.e. no topic is set but the conversation is allowed to follow its own spontaneous directions. The session can be considerably improved by directing the last part of it : if, after 45 minutes of undirected discussion, a highly provocative topic of general interest—an emotional bomb—is tossed into the group for 10–15 minutes vivid high-tempo discussion.

The W.O.S.B. Progressive Group Task—an outdoor task involving the management of men and materials— is unorganised but directed. The task includes several sub-tasks or obstacles of progressive difficulty and increasing frustration. Tasks will naturally be related to the field of activity for which men are being selected. If they are to be soldiers, the testing pattern may include physical outdoor tasks though these are not indispensable, or even necessary: if they are to be civil servants, group discussions or planning projects will be more relevant.

The Human Problems Session—where the candidates took it in turns to act the parts of officer and 'stooge' discussing the latter's problem in an interview—had a Leaderless Group background. Like another important variant, the outdoor task with a designated leader, the Human Problems Session gave the selectors an opportunity to gain a clearer impression of a particular individual. Indeed, Dr Harris believed that 'this was possibly the most valuable single technique in W.O.S.B. procedure. One which could give more useful information in a given time than any other: though, being but one item in the entire observational field, it must of course be related to the rest of the evidence.' (p. 125).

What did the Stress Group Task, in its various guises, reveal? The answer of course is that this depended on what the selectors were looking for. In the early W.O.S.B. there appears to have been a strong emphasis on the value of the Stress Group Task for revealing those who were naturally 'group-cohesive' or 'group-disruptive'. Stress, it was hoped, would bare the candidate's degree of stability, that 'mental stamina' without which he could not bind the group together to face the external or internal threats of disintegration, and without which he could not accept and use his own inner anxiety in the moments of *impasse* or crisis to both understand and act with sympathy towards his men.

At a distance of over 20 years, it is possible to criticise some of the points of emphasis in the early W.O.S.B. doctrine, and also some of the experimental techniques which enjoyed a brief summer of popularity in the late 1940's. Certainly many of the individual tests, questionnaires and interviews which made up the rest of the three day board have long since been improved out of all recognition. But the essential contribution of W.O.S.B.—the functional understanding of leadership and its use as a selection device of the small group with a task to perform—have proved enormously successful. Even by 1949 this method had been adopted by the Royal Air Force, and by the French and Belgian Armies. In 1962 I was shown a number of small group obstacles erected by the officer selection wing of the United States Marine Corps at Quantico, Virginia, and the colonel in command informed me that he had visited a W.O.S.B. in England some years earlier to make drawings for them. In this country the ending of National Service reduced the need for a number of W.O.S.B's and only one has been retained, now known as the R.C.B. (Regular Commissions Board), which is situated at Westbury in Wiltshire. In the non-military sphere, the Civil Service, many large firms such as Unilever Ltd., and the Church of England, have adopted the W.O.S.B. approach, and adapted it with varying degrees of success.

One important question remains. How far are psychiatrists and psychologists necessary in leadership selection boards? Dr Harris expressed the view more than once in his book that their help was essential at future W.O.S.B.'s, and in designing tests; he clearly assumed that there would be scientists of both kinds available at future conferences. In favour of this opinion we may note that leadership selection boards may easily lose their character and revert to the old interviewing, or subjective 'talent-spotting' methods where there is no one present on the staff with a firm grasp of the essential theory and the principles of applying it for that purpose. Only a historian, for example, would today be able to trace much connection between the Church of England A.C.C.M. (Advisory Council for the Church's Ministry) selection week-ends, and the early W.O.S.B's, or even the present R.C.B., and this is so even when full allowances have been made for the necessary changes in method. Secondly, the psychological testing of individuals for intelligence, interests, aptitudes and relevant personality factors must remain largely the preserve of the professional. If not actually administering the tests he must retain a close watch on the way they are used and the conclusions which are drawn from them. In both these fields when professional help is withdrawn there tends to be a gradual invasion of old assumptions about leadership which may be still luxuriant in the remaining 95 per cent of the sponsoring organisation, just as a clearing in a forest abandoned by the first pioneers will be slowly overgrown until it becomes indistinguishable from its surrounds.

There are, however, two factors against the continued employment of psychologists and psychiatrists by organisations to select leaders. In the first place, their long professional training makes them expensive to hire. Secondly, they tend to import other sectors of their professional interests into the work in hand. In the case of Dr Harris, a group psychotherapist, this is evident from the many pages in his book which reflect his academic and practical interest in his chosen specialisation, such as his attempts to relate the individual's behaviour in a small group to personality categories (schizoid, hysteric etc.) and his concern for giving therapeutic help at W.O.S.B's where possible (p. 191). The group psychologist, or psychotherapist may also consciously or unconsciously import into a board selecting leaders for an organisation, his own assumptions about the rôle of a leader (based perhaps on the rôle of the therapist in a discussion group of mentally maladjusted individuals) which are inappropriate to the characteristic working situation of the organisation or institution in question. For example, Dr Harris' composite description of a 'group-cohesive' individual (pp. 92–93) does not correspond in several respects to that of a platoon commander on the battlefield.

Thus the leadership selection area requires a marriage of two kinds of knowledge : social psychological (A), and practical experience of the command in the characteristic working situation (B), making together AB. The professional psychotherapist can often only contribute AA, just as the practising leader can only offer BB. In fact, W.O.S.B. was the child of A and B, and it is a matter of regret that we still await the official history of this most exciting creation, a chronicle which would no doubt give the B elements their just place and enable us to see the experiment more in perspective. It is usually the A contributors who write the books !

In my own view, a leadership selection conference or training course may be likened to the design of an industrial machine, which must be constructed so that it meets the needs of the organisation and yet is simple enough to be operated by a person with less theoretical knowledge and technological know-how than the inventor. So the professional group psychologist and psychiatrist can evolve a selection or training scheme in dialogue with the organisation's practitioners which can be run by others in that particular field with a given level of training. This implies that there will be enough men in the organisation with sufficient natural aptitude and professional experience to act as selectors or trainers, and secondly, that the length of time necessary to train them in A knowledge and skills is acceptable to the organisation. The 'expert' can then simply keep a watching brief on the conference or course, just as a firm which sells a computer to an organisation might remain responsible for maintaining this complex piece of equipment. The fact that R.C.B. today can be staffed by officers seconded from ordinary units without losing its overall effectiveness speaks much for the work of the early experimenters. In this case, however, a small number of professional psychologists at the Defence Operational Analysis Establishment in Surrey remain responsible for certain aspects of the R.C.B.s design, such as the invention of new group task obstacles.

In the light of the successful application of the functional understanding of leadership to the problem of *selection* the reader may well wonder whether or not any attempts were made to apply the same group approach to the more difficult task of leadership *training*. In fact, one such experiment was made during the Second World War. This deserves consideration in this chapter, partly because it stands close in time to the early W.O.S.B. 'trial runs', and secondly because it never quite divested itself of a 'selection' flavour.

On 16 March 1943 General Sir Ronald Adam decided to open a special leadership training school for those who had gained (usually on the grounds of immaturity) a 'Not Yet' verdict from W.O.S.B. Eleven weeks later the school opened at Poolewe in Wester Ross, with its purpose suitably disguised by the title 'Highland Fieldcraft Training Centre', and with Lord Rowallan as its first Commanding Officer.

The chief merit of the H.F.T.C. lay in the fact that during its ten week course it provided the participants with plenty of outdoor work in small groups, with specific tasks to perform. These were somewhat similar to natural primitive hunting groups, and they provided a concentrated dose of practical group experience which could, and did, develop latent leadership talent. An especially valuable feature was the re-arrangement of groups at regular intervals, which made the candidates go through the important process of adjusting themselves to others not once but several times. On average, rather more than two-thirds of the students passed W.O.S.B. after their ten weeks course (868 out of 1,286 in just over one year).

Perhaps the most serious limitation of the course as leadership training, was the apparent failure of the staff to appreciate the important new *theory* which lay behind the W.O.S.B. technique. They still thought of leadership in terms of inherent qualities and therefore offered no instruction on the nature of the small group and the functions needed within it. Only the sociometric technique of asking each member of the group to place the others in order of leadership-merit seems to have been borrowed from W.O.S.B. In the tenth week selectors from W.O.S.B. would also attend the course, which must have reinforced its selection atmosphere.

Many ingredients went into the H.F.T.C. pudding, notably Scouting (derived from Lord Rowallan), Character Training on the lines of Kurt Hahn's school at Gordonstoun, and Battle Schools, which at this time were stimulating a more imaginative approach to field exercises. Perhaps because the staff were not conversant with the research developments in their subject, they tended (like the group psychotherapists at W.O.S.B.) to bring too much of their own 'luggage' with them. Hence the students received instruction in such subjects as botany, astronomy, arms-training, make and mend of clothing, first-aid, bayonet combat, boxing, rock climbing, and the use of explosives! As Chief Scout after the war, Lord Rowallan wrote to some old course members, 'Of course the great problem was to disguise from you the fact that it was Scouting . . .'[2]

Therefore only in a somewhat accidental sense could the H.F.T.C. be described as an application of the functional approach to the problem of leadership training. Rather the course should be regarded as a development of Boy Scouting, with more mature groups than the usual patrols, operating in situations fraught with some degree of stress or danger. Membership of five working groups in ten weeks with an officer leader, whose example could be observed and then emulated by the candidates themselves in practice command appointments, could only stimulate leadership potential. But much of what passed as leadership training was, in fact, only an extended form of selection. This appreciation of both the good and weak points of the H.F.T.C. may also be held to apply to a much smaller extent to its linear descendants, the Outward Bound Trust Schools.[3] Certainly the achievement in leadership training was not in the same order as that in the field of selection, where W.O.S.B. represented a real 'break-through' which was achieved by the application of intelligence and research to the solution of a pressing practical problem.

CHAPTER FOUR

LEADERSHIP TRAINING

From the previous pages it is clear that the functional approach to leadership has been applied successfully to the problem of *selecting* military leaders, but not at all (in a conscious way) to the more difficult task of *training* them. In this chapter and the following two I shall describe how this has been done during the last six years at the Royal Military Academy Sandhurst. Readers who are primarily interested in developing leadership potential in other fields than the military will find here a concrete example of how general principles can be applied to meet the needs of a particular organisation. Of course the application will be different in other situations, but the principles themselves do not change.

First, however, in order to 'set the scene', a word about Sandhurst. At present an officer cadet enters the R.M.A.S. at the age of 18 or 19 years, either after attaining the necessary academic standards and passing R.C.B. or (in a minority of cases) after completing a course at the Army School, Welbeck. He joins the Academy with about 260 other officer cadets, who together form a numbered intake (e.g. Intake 39). On arrival the intake is divided among three colleges (Old, New and Victory) and then further sub-divided into the four companies which together make up a college. These junior company intakes (usually of 20–23 cadets) spend their first of six terms at the R.M.A.S. upon purely military basic training. Terms 2 to 5 are a mixture of academic and military studies, with the former predominant. As the senior intake in their last term the officer cadets again devote all their time to military studies, and in addition play a key part in the administration of their companies as Under Officers, Cadet Sergeants, Corporals and Senior Cadets.

Now looking at the Academy as a whole (and this is equally true of many other organisations with the development of leadership potential as one of their aims) we could say that there are five overlapping areas in which the actual quality of leadership training is determined.

The Five Areas of Leadership Training

These are listed not in the order of importance—they are all equal as far as that is concerned—but in terms of the numbers involved, from virtually the whole Academy down to a very few individuals.

> Structure.
> Leadership Course.
> Field Leadership Training.
> Staff Training.
> Research and Advisory Unit.

In order to make it clear what these stand for, let us now consider each in turn.

Structure

Within terms of the present 'structure' there are two aspects of perennial importance as far as the development of leadership goes; the general ethos of Sandhurst, and the number and variety of opportunities which exist for officer cadets to practise leadership.

Atmosphere, by its very nature, is difficult to analyse and almost impossible to convey to others. The pink-white building of Old College, guarded by those six gleaming brass guns taken at Waterloo, the Chapel lined with memorials to fallen officers, the traditional parades and ceremonies of the Academy : all these exercise their own pervasive influence. Moreover, careful attention has always been paid to the selection of those officers and N.C.O.s who come to Sandhurst as instructors for three-year tours of duty. This means that officer cadets who, like all young people, are naturally and keenly observant, can learn much by seeing good examples in the course of their everyday military studies.

The personal relationships in the place—between officer and officer, officer and N.C.O., and both with the cadet—create a potent natural influence, the more so because it is not usually conscious.

Nor should the influence of cadet upon cadet be forgotten. An eminent soldier has underlined the importance of such contacts : 'At most schools and training centres the relationship with one's contemporaries is the most potent influence. Only when one starts to work with older people does one really start to absorb their influence. That has been my experience, anyway. I learnt from those who taught me when young because they had authority over me. I do not think example meant much—indeed the example of the teacher or instructor was often rejected because of an antagonism to his rôle. Example was absorbed from friends, relations and admired contemporaries'.

This aspect, the importance of staff and fellow cadets personifying leadership qualities, or, in other words, setting an example, should be self-evident. Any approach to leadership training which did not stress this 'area' would rightly strike the informed reader as being at least narrow and possibly doctrinaire.

Again much of the education and training in the six term course contributes to leadership development, without this being explicitly stated or spelt out for the officer cadet. His whole military course is designed to give him the *knowledge* required to perform the task functions required in a platoon or troop in a wide variety of situations. A mastery of map reading, for example, gives the officer cadet the skills necessary to lead a group across country towards its objective : if the platoon commander cannot read a map, or use a compass accurately, the task will not be achieved, and team maintenance will suffer accordingly. It might be instructive to consider some other components of the Sandhurst course from the leadership angle :

Tactics: the ways in which a company or platoon can be led to achieve its task on the battlefield.

Weapon-training: necessary technical knowledge for the leader.

Signals: mastery of wireless as a means of giving and receiving orders and information between military groups.

Physical exercise: the leader needs to be as fit as possible in order to lead the group in exacting outdoor tasks.

Military law: knowledge of the fabric of formal laws and standards which help bind the armed forces together as a cohesive whole and thereby enable them to fulfil their purposes.

'Methods of instruction': an introduction to the leader's work as a teacher, an element in most leadership rôles, and a prominent one in that of the officers, especially in peace time.

70

Academic studies—e.g. languages, mathematics and science, current affairs—also contribute to the background knowledge required by the military leader in the modern army. The main aim of the Military History Department, for example, is to teach officer cadets the broad outlines of 'les transformations de la guerre' : some knowledge in fact of his profession in the depth which history can give. Secondly, the officer cadet looks at some of the formative experiences of the British Army since the days of Marlborough. The officer cadet is preparing to join a 'family' and therefore needs to know the family history. (The powerful idea of the 'family' is a strong group-cohesive force in any organisation, but it may not have originated for that reason. Possibly its beginnings may be found in the days when the tribe or clan, a cluster of families, was also the main hunting or fighting unit. Perhaps where a 'work' group enjoys a prolonged existence, it tends to take into itself some of the characteristics of the family.) Thirdly, the Military History course sets out to give the officer cadet an opportunity of gaining an insight into minds of great commanders, an aim which can perhaps be achieved best by encouraging a wide reading of biographies and memoirs, such as Field Marshal Viscount Slim's *Defeat into Victory*.

The fourth purpose of the Military History syllabus is to provide officer cadets with an opportunity to apply the principles of good instruction and to practise leadership. In each of the three 'phases' within the obligatory 112 periods of Military History, the company intake is divided into four syndicates of five or six cadets under an appointed leader. One of the four then 'presents' a campaign or battle to the rest of the college intake (80–90 cadets) and the other three put on their presentation to the smaller audience of their own company intake. By this means some 144 out of an Academy intake of 280 officer cadets (or 12 out of a company intake of 22) have the chance of leading a small group, i.e. to define its aim, make a plan, obtain the necessary knowledge of the resources, maintain the syndicate as a working team in the face of many distractions, and take into account the individual gifts or limitations of their fellow members. The success or failure of the presentation is a yardstick of how well they have performed these functions.

The provision of such leadership opportunities within the Academy is a vital element of its 'structure'. Of course the normal range of tactical training in the field allows many to act as platoon commanders, sergeants, or section leaders, and as care is taken to record these appointments no cadet can fail to hold at least one such command (and usually many more) during his two years at the R.M.A.S. But just as W.O.S.B. sought to place the candidate for a commission in groups with different tasks in order to observe his *range,* so it is important in training to extend the officer cadet by also allowing him to lead in a variety of groups and situations. For the insights gained in other group situations may well be relevant, if only as a minor theme, in his characteristic rôle of platoon commander in peace and war. Therefore breadth of group opportunity is an essential part of leadership education, and all similar programmes should perhaps include it.

For in nurturing leadership growth one may use the best fertilisers, but unless there is light and room for growth, little will be achieved. To some extent we can analyse the key elements in that synthesis of light and space, but much remains opaque. It is, however, a matter of prime importance in any organisation or institution concerned with leadership development to be aware of the all-pervading influence of 'structure' in its broadest sense, and its ability to speak to the student at a deeper level, possibly even in contradiction to what the official teachers are saying or doing. Of course, an organisation is more effective if the degree of contradiction is reduced to the inescapable minimum.

The Leadership Course

Any organisation concerned with leadership training conveys to its students some theory or set of notions about the nature of leadership. ['Theory' is used here in its primary sense as 'supposition explaining something, especially one based on principles independent of the phenomena etc. to be explained' (*Concise Oxford Dictionary*), not in its secondary sense of 'speculative view ... often implying fancifulness'.] This may be implicit. One sometimes finds that those who claim not to entertain any 'abstract' ideas about leadership in fact hold the *qualities* approach as an unexamined and largely unconscious assumption which is then passed on almost accidentally to others with neither bearer nor receiver being entirely aware of the process. Even an institution which taught nothing in a formal sense to its junior members about the nature of leadership would in reality be advertising a theory, namely that there is nothing worth teaching.

In contrast to this last extreme view, most organisations which set out to develop leadership feel obliged to offer some explicit or formal instruction on the subject. For the purposes of this book we may call this the Leadership Course. Such courses vary much from organisation to organisation in terms of aims, content, length and methods of education. Each of these will be considered in turn. First, however, let me state what I believe to be perhaps the fundamental principle of all explicit leadership training, namely *that theory and practice should mutually inter-act upon each other*. In other words, there should be a dialogue between what is learnt as theory and what is undergone as practical experience. This may take many forms. The student may, for example, try to apply theory to the understanding of a practical leadership problem, or he may find that certain aspects of his experience illumines what he had previously known only as an abstract concept. We may see this dialogue at work in other fields, where nature informed by intelligence and experience becomes art. The interaction of an artist's natural ability and the laws of perspective will lead him to draw better, or his anatomical knowledge will influence (and be influenced by) his observation and depiction of the human body. Therefore, to improve on nature we must bring understanding to bear upon experience.

Having chosen the appropriate theory there remains the purely educational problems of teaching it. In order to show how these may be overcome, it is necessary to describe an actual course, which will be done in the following chapter. Here it is possible only to lay down two principles which will be illustrated later :
1. that the relation of theory to practice should *begin* during the formal syllabus,
2. that the methods of education employed should be appropriate to the aims of the course.

Field Leadership Training

Most organisations concerned with developing leadership potential provide their students with some opportunity of 'taking charge' in a near-characteristic working situation. 'Field Leadership Training' implies any situation in which the leader is in some sense still in *statu pupillari*, where his activities are to be commented upon with the aim of improving his leadership performance.

From the view point of the student in the leadership rôle, the most important requirement is to know how effective his leadership has been, and to understand why he has succeeded or failed. To some extent the degree of task performance will give him a rough and ready measure, but this needs to be supplemented by reactions or 'feed back' from an experienced instructor and also from the other members of the group. The giving of such reactions—which depend for their quality upon the *awareness* of the group, their *understanding* of needs and functions, and their *skill* in commenting—also forms a major plank in the training of those members who are not in the leadership rôle at the given time. They are learning by the critical appreciation of concrete examples, by applying theory to understand the practice of others. If no such opportunities exist already in an organisation, then they may have to be created. Fortunately, at the R.M.A. Sandhurst frequent tactical exercises which reach their climax in bi-annual periods of ten days overseas training, when officer cadets from the senior intake held command appointments over juniors, have long served as ready-made opportunities for taking leadership out of the classroom and into the field. The results of some experiments in that context will be recounted in a later chapter, and again they may serve as a 'case study' for other organisations who want to get the best out of the practical experience they make possible for their junior leaders.

Staff Training

From what has already been written about both the formal syllabus and field leadership training, it will be clear that much depends upon the quality and training of the staff for this kind of work. The ideal instructor should possess natural ability and experience as a leader in his own sphere, a working knowledge of the general theory of leadership at a greater depth and width than the level on which he is expected to teach, and reasonable skill in a variety of educational methods. Few people possess all three qualifications in the same high degree. But although much of the creative work in designing training programmes may be done by two or more minds working together, committees do not make good teachers.

In the majority of cases the only practical solution is to choose as instructors men or women with the first type of experience and to add on to it specialist training in the rôle of a leadership trainer. But a high order of ability as a leader is not a guarantee of success as a leadership trainer : the two rôles are inter-related yet not identical. There will always be a small proportion of instructors who naturally perceive the distinction and adapt accordingly; a majority of the others may be trained for the job providing they possess enquiring minds which are open to new ideas and new ways of doing things without losing their critical faculties.

The degree of knowledge and experience in all three senses possessed by the prospective instructors is a key factor in determining the content and shape of the syllabus. By the provision of common written and visual material, and by the careful selection of educational methods, a minimum standard can be achieved throughout an organisation's training programme. And so the employment of professionals in *designing* a course can dramatically mitigate the mistakes of a poor teacher (and, incidentally, give the new instructor the confidence of knowing that all does not rest on his shoulders). But above that minimum much depends upon the natural or acquired ability of the instructor, and the quality of the training made available to him will be a vital factor in deciding the level of his performance.

Research and Advisory Staff

The effective employment of staff with many other general duties in the specialist rôle of leadership instructors both on the formal syllabus or for field training presupposes the existence of a *specialist* research and advisory staff, who would keep the four areas discussed already above under a regular surveillance with the aim of improving the quality of implicit or explicit leadership education in each. This entails research into relevant developments in social psychology, education and professional leadership training, especially in organisations with similar purposes to one's own. This also means making available the results of one's own research into leadership training, so that there is a continuous dialogue between organisations with a strong mutual interest in developing the full potential of young leaders. For in this, as in any other educational field, research and teaching go hand in hand. This is perhaps especially true in an evolving area of education such as leadership training : laurels, like cut flowers, soon fade.

Summary

It would be invidious to place the above five areas in any sort of order. They are all important and all related to each other either in formal or informal ways, so that improvement in one area should affect the others. It is important, however, to separate them in this way if only to give the reader the opportunity to assess how far *his* organisation is meeting the necessary requirements in each area. Together they form the essential framework for any effective leadership training programme.

CHAPTER FIVE

THE LEADERSHIP SYLLABUS

In this chapter the focus is on one of the five areas of leadership training previously listed : the Leadership Syllabus. Its purpose is to give a concrete example of one way in which the functional approach to leadership is at present being taught, thereby illustrating the principles which have just been enumerated.

Until 1963 the formal syllabus at the R.M.A.S. was based on the *qualities approach* (see pp. 11–13), not as a matter of conscious choice, but because no alternative was known at that time. The syllabus was divided as follows :

Term 3

Period
1. Introduction and Major Qualities of Leadership.
2. Qualities of Military Leadership.
3. The Elements of High Morale.

Term 4

4. Discipline.
5. Leadership and Loyalty (including problems).
6. Man Management—Object, Principles and Major Aspects.

Term 5

7. and 8. Problems in Man Management.
9. Problems in the Maintenance of Morale in Peace and War.
10. Life as an Officer within the Regiment (Officers' Mess, Sergeants' Mess, Social Occasions, Games etc.).
11. Life as an Officer (A reminder of some conventions).

Term 6

12.   Film *Officers and Men*.
13.   Talk by Academy Sergeant Major.

There were three major weaknesses in this syllabus. First, the *qualities approach*, for reasons already given, did not provide a satisfactory basis for discussion. Secondly, the instructors found it difficult to maintain interest, and tended to occupy more and more of the discussion themselves introducing stories from their own experience, to enliven the proceedings. This tendency towards a monologue, or at least an instructor-centred pattern, was increased by the room arrangement, as shown here :

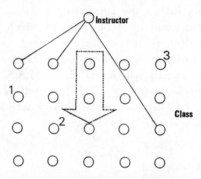

1. INSTRUCTOR-CENTRED TEACHING

In this diagram the instructor is standing in front of his audience and either addressing all of them (dotted arrow) or engaging in question-and-answer dialogue with class members. Note that the 'lines of communication' range out from him like the spokes of a wheel. Conversely there tends to be very little lateral communication, e.g. from 1 to 3. Where this is not expressly prohibited (in many school lessons, for example), it is not helped by the physical facts that 2 cannot see 3's face, and 1 would have to twist round in his seat to talk to 2. It is difficult to address the back of someone's head. Therefore the room arrangement discouraged discussion.

The third weakness rested in the assumption that before the officer cadet could fruitfully discuss leadership, he must be given the 'answers', namely the authoritative opinions of prominent generals. Therefore before each of these 45 minute periods the instructor would ensure that the officer cadet read up the relevant passages in *Serve to Lead,* a Sandhurst anthology of extracts on Leadership, Morale, Discipline and Man-Management. As a result the officer cadets simply regurgitated the views of Field Marshal This and General That to his company commander. The periods sometimes became little more than a memory test to see whether the accepted list of qualities had been safely learnt. This approach did not, of course, encourage the officer cadet to think for himself : his thinking had been done for him by some celebrated soldier, and all he had to do was to produce the answers which would please his company commander—the acceptable solutions.

These views were confirmed in 1962 by giving 140 officer cadets in Intake 30 a questionnaire on leadership training to complete just before they left Sandhurst. To the question 'How helpful has the Leadership Syllabus been?' a variety of answers were given, which could be roughly broken down into the following categories :

Very helpful :	14%
Some help :	36%
Little help	25%
No help or no answer :	25%

Many found the lectures 'over their heads', and became bored. Some were bored by their company commander's personal anecdotes. Many felt the subject should be treated with greater urgency. Some regarded the tuition as too basic—'the same old stuff', but others found most value in the discussion of specific problems (i.e. lessons 7 and 8). 'Next to useless' was one comment. It could also be deduced that the 50 per cent who were getting little or nothing from the syllabus were the more average and low average cadets, precisely those who needed the most guidance.

After three years of research, discussion and experiment, the old syllabus was recast into the following form :

Period

Term 3

1. to 9.   Concentrated course on the Functional Approach to Leadership.

10.   Qualities of Military Leadership.

Term 4

11. and 12.   Discipline.

13. and 14.   Loyalty and its problems.

79

15. and 16.   Morale.

Term 5

17. and 18.   Problems of Individuals.

19.   Talk by Academy Sergeant Major.

The concentrated course of nine periods, lasting usually from 10.45 a.m. until 12.30 p.m. on the following day, is designed to stimulate constructive thought about the subject of leadership, and to introduce the officer cadet to the functional aspects of it, thus contributing to the overall aim of the leadership syllabus, which was defined as follows :

... to make each cadet aware of the nature and practice of leadership so that he can apply his talents to the command of men with confidence and understanding.

To these ends certain important changes in the methods of education were introduced. As the course has already served as a model for others in non-military fields it will now be described in some detail.

Session 1. Introduction

Description

After a brief introductory talk upon the aims and shape of the course, the instructor sticks up a large sheet of white paper bearing a question such as 'What is leadership?' or 'What does a leader do in order to lead?' He divides the company intake of approximately 20 officer cadets into syndicates of five or six, which then separate out of earshot of each other, and discuss the question for about 45 minutes. When that time has elapsed the instructor re-assembles them, and asks for a verbal report from each syndicate, and while the individual spokesmen recount their main points, he writes them down on four sheets of paper. With the written reports displayed by fastening them on to a convenient wall with pressure tape so that they can be moved easily, the officer cadets are invited to compare them, looking for common ground, or examining differences of view between the four groups. The instructor 'seals off' the discussion when time is up, without offering more than a very general summary of the officer cadets' opinions, and the position that has been reached after the plenary part of the session. Either he, or a company officer who is acting as an observer on the course, then hands to each officer cadet a reaction sheet which has to be completed immediately.

Comments
1. *The Group Approach to Learning.* In contrast to the pattern shown in diagram 1, we may represent this session by two others, one showing the syndicates at work discussing the set question, and the second the plenary last phase.

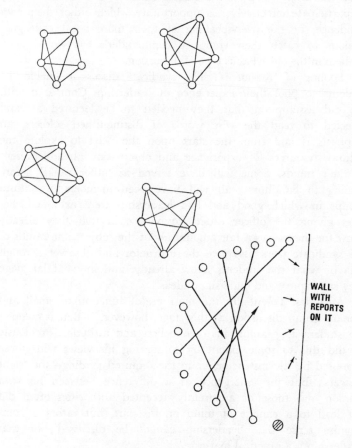

WALL
WITH
REPORTS
ON IT

2. SYNDICATE AND PLENARY DISCUSSION

From the lines of communication on these diagrams it may be seen that the arrangement of the students is designed to enable them to talk to each other; it is essentially a picture of *dialogue* rather than *monologue*. In the context of leadership training why are such patterns preferable? We may adduce three reasons:

(a) Participation. Instead of sitting like sheep passively listening to a long talk, or responding to spoken questions, the students are at once involved in the course. They are confronted with the task of framing a joint answer, and therefore must make some decisions which will be publicly examined. Moreover the small syndicate discussion gives the quieter officer cadets an opportunity to participate effectively; an opportunity which either their own diffidence, or the over-speaking of their more vocal colleagues anxious to catch their company commander's eye would deny to them in the old syllabus type of discussion.

(b) Pooling of 'Resources'. The syndicate discussion enable the students to pool their experience of leadership. Compared with the old assumption that they needed to be lectured at, and directed to read the wise words of distinguished soldiers, an emphasis is laid from the start upon the need to explore the natural 'resources' of experience and observation already present in their minds. Some will have served as 'other ranks' before coming to Sandhurst; all will have been members of natural groups in which good and bad leadership were exhibited. Besides giving the officer cadets confidence in that they already know for themselves a fair amount about the subject, the results of the syndicate work also give the instructor and observer a rough idea of what the students know already, and in what language they can express and understand ideas.

(c) Attitudes. Potentially the most useful function of small and plenary group discussion at this stage, however, is that it compels the student to examine his own beliefs and attitudes. Previously he did this to some extent by comparing his views with those expressed by the instructor, or in the required reading—the 'right answers'. But the emergence of a difference between his own opinion and those of apparently accepted authorities often did not lead to a change of mind on his part, but rather a compromise sense that 'leadership cannot be discussed', or that 'leadership is a practical matter'.

In this session the student's assumptions about leadership are exposed to friendly appraisal by his fellows, who may challenge him, for example, to produce evidence or examples to illustrate his statements. The syndicate reports in the plenary phase, when placed side by side, may reveal quite different views which will serve to deepen the question 'What is leadership?' in the student's mind. He will see that his own considered conclusion is not the final answer, that there is still an area open for enquiry and reflection. In other words, the ground of his mind will be ploughed up and opened to the reception of new ideas : he will have been *thinking* for himself.

2. *The Instructor's Rôle.* The instructor's primary task is to create an atmosphere in which the student can work to maximum effect upon the problem in hand. This means that he must diminish some of the unseen pressures which may inhibit a true exchange of ideas. Just as the functional method of leadership selection includes about 10 per cent of (unintended) training, so a concentrated course will embrace a small element of assessment, but this should not enter into the formal purpose, and as far as possible the instructor should put this aspect out of his mind. For nothing freezes discussion more, or produces a crop of stultified 'right answers' than if the students feel that they are being watched. Similarly, the instructors should not show by any overt action, such as a half-smile or a nod, that he agrees with any one view, as this may well set everyone off on the game of trying to find the answers which will please him : a kind of 'Blind Man's Buff'. On the contrary, he should be setting an important group standard by listening with genuine interest to even the least promising contributions, and confine his interventions to questions at appropriate moments. Giving is better than receiving, but sometimes we can give most only by receiving. The instructor must not only hear what is said, he must listen to the intentions behind the words of the speaker without losing his awareness of the other students.

3. *Evaluation.* At the end of the session the students are issued with a questionnaire which they are asked to complete and hand in immediately without writing their names at the top. It might contain the following questions (with suitable spaces between them for answers) :

1. How would you rate this session?
Poor (0); Average (40); Good (60); Very Good (80); Excellent (100)
2. Which part did you prefer?
3. What in particular have you learnt?
4. Any other comments?

The purpose of three-fold. In the first place it allows the individual four or five quiet minutes to mull over in his mind what has been said and to pick out the points of most value to himself, which, of course, may not be the same as those selected by another officer cadet. What he has seen or understood more clearly must then be crystallised into words.

Secondly, these reaction sheets give the instructor a more accurate picture of what the students are feeling or thinking as individuals at any given point in the course. And thirdly, the collected reaction sheets from all the companies give the Leadership Committee (i.e. the Research and Advisory Staff) some measure of how successful the course has been, and how the students believe that it may be improved.

On the whole, reactions to the first session tend to be mixed. Some rate it low because they believe that the intake has failed to reach any common conclusions, and their morale has correspondingly fallen. Sometimes they blame the instructor for not enlightening them. This may be especially true of those students who have become dependent on 'teacher' to supply them with satisfying answers, and his apparent 'withdrawal' occasions some stress. Often the instructor can in part allay these anxieties by pointing out at the end of Session 1 that the remainder of the course is designed to shed light on the questions that have been raised and discussed. A majority of students, however, will respond by welcoming the chance to think for themselves.

Session 2. Observation Exercise

Description

After a short break the students re-assemble. The instructor then gives a 20 minute talk on the research findings on leadership in the past 30 years, working from the qualities approach to the twin concepts of *group needs* and *functional leadership*. When any clarifying questions have been answered, the officer cadets go outside for an Observation Skill Exercise. Briefly, while one syndicate tackles an outdoor physical task along Regular Commissions Board lines, the other three observe the functions which are being performed in it to meet the areas of need, i.e. to accomplish the task, to maintain the working relationships of the team, and to respond to any particular individual need. After the findings have been discussed, another syndicate tackles a second task, and the observations continue until the time is up.

Comments

1. *Purpose.* The aim of the session is to offer the student an alternative way of looking at leadership than that contained in the qualities approach, namely the concept of functional leadership. As some, if not all, of the syndicates will have already produced a set of leadership qualities in answer to the first question asked them, and by process of comparing their four reports found that there is little agreement even amongst themselves on a definitive list, they will find some support in the fact that research as a whole supports their own conclusions, and be 'open' to a new approach. Having explored (and probably exhausted) their own resources they are ready for the ideas of others, providing they are backed by some evidence. The diagram of the three overlapping circles (see p. 18) provides a welcome visual illustration, the basis of a 'sketch map' which will linger in the mind.

2. *Observation.* The session gives the students an immediate opportunity to put theory into practice by using it to observe a group in action. They may have followed the explanation of the functional approach conceptually, and even understood it, but the only test of how far they have truly grasped the theory is whether they can use it. Therefore when it comes to the students giving their observations, the instructor should not be too surprised if at least half of them reveal that they have not comprehended the main idea of functional leadership. Indeed, the first part of the Observation Skill Exercise may be seen as an extension of the 20 minute lecturette.

In the latter stages of the exercise, however, the students should become *aware* of the group they are observing, of the relationships within it, and the processes by which it works. In particular they should begin to *understand* the functions required from the designated leader if the task is to be achieved, and the cohesiveness of the team maintained.

3. *Variations.* In the first 'trial run' led by myself, with a group of 15 officer cadets drawn from different companies, one of the syndicates acted as committee with a decision to make, while the others sat around and observed the task and team maintenance functions. The present outdoor obstacles were substituted for the committee problem for two reasons. First, in order to arrange

and lead the session effectively in that shape the company commanders would have needed much more specialist training as instructors than it was feasible to expect at that time. Secondly, it was felt that the picture of the leader acting as chairman of a discussion group might linger as an image of how all military decisions should be taken. Therefore, in light of the need to make the course as foolproof as possible, it was decided to drop it. In other than junior military courses these factors do not apply.

4. *The Instructor's Role.* Given a clear and simple brief the 20 minute talk should present no problems to the instructor. The Observation Skill Exercise, however, is not easy to direct. Although the administrative details of the session, e.g. the briefing of the syndicate leader who has to attempt the physical task, may be delegated to the officer observer, who now becomes a co-trainer, the instructor in the observation phase still has to note for himself the important functions performed or omitted in the task syndicate, while at the same time keeping an eye on the student observers. This is necessary because in the early stages, before the officer cadets have understood what they are there to do, they tend to 'identify' themselves with their fellows doing the task, and to think up the ways in which they would solve it. Sometimes, of course, when the syndicate being observed gets into a hopeless and humorous muddle, it is more human to laugh with them than maintain a dispassionate detachment, but for the most part the audience should not get absorbed in the practical solutions of any given problem but rather in *their* task, which is the observation of what the leader does to get his team to achieve its aim.

In the plenary discussion phase after each task, when observations are given by the students, the instructor's rôle is again to set and maintain certain group standards, notably that comments should 'speak to data'. Instead of making vague remarks, such as 'Jones was a good leader', or 'Jones held the group together', the students should be able to collect information, and therefore support their views with some evidence (which may, of course, be interpreted differently by others). To help them to select significant data an observation sheet is issued to them with key functions listed upon it which a leader of a group faced with a simple physical task might be expected to perform. This sheet is based upon a list of leadership functions given out and discussed at the end of the 20 minute lecturette. [See Appendix B.

86

This list, compiled by the author and a number of officers on field training in Cyprus (1962), is only a guide, and is not designed to cover all the functions required in every situation.]

The discipline of 'speaking to data' also encourages the officer cadet to be objective in his general approach to the study of leadership. By accurately reading the visible 'effects' of a leader's actions he can begin to understand (with the help of the general theory condensed for him on the observation sheet) some of the invisible 'causes', such as the commission or omission of some vital leadership function. Moreover the fact that other members of the observer group may appear to *see* more than he does, or to see it in a different light, may serve to convince him that his awareness, understanding and skill in perceiving what is happening in a leadership situation are limited and can be developed. During this phase the instructor should resist the temptation to give his own more experienced and complete observations, and allow the observer group to piece together their own picture with the help of the syndicate who have attempted the task, and who can therefore to a certain extent verify or refute some of the observations made. The instructor's job is again to make the group as a whole explore its own resources of recent observation and experience, to allow the officer cadets to teach each other, and to use his own observations only to illustrate the standard of 'speaking to data' if necessary.

5. *Evaluation.* On the whole this session is rated highly by participants, and a majority usually understand the concept of functional leadership in varying degrees by the end of it, but not all will have accepted it, even as a working hypothesis. Again, however, the practical approach underlying the observation method will have provoked more thought, and guided it to some possible conclusions.

Section 3. Military Leadership

Description

The purpose of this session is to bridge the gap between non-military and military leadership. In a short talk the instructor emphasises the influence of the characteristic working situation, and the aims of the organisation upon the degree to which the leader can share decisions with subordinates. Military groups operating in the extreme stress situation of the battlefield both need and expect strong leadership from one man. Then the students are again divided up to discuss the factors which effect group participation in decision-making and other key leadership functions. When the syndicate reports have been stuck on the wall, and compared by the plenary gathering, the instructor may then use a modified form of the 'Decision-making Continuum' shown above on p. 23, to bind the discussion together. Then he may perhaps summarise the three sessions so far by suggesting that the good leader should be always *aware* of task, team maintenance and individual requirements; he should have sufficient *understanding* to know what functions are necessary at a given time, and lastly, he should possess the *skill* and the training either to perform them himself, or to ensure that someone else does under his guidance.

Comments

1. *General.* This session allows the officer cadet to focus his attention upon the importance of the *situation*, both in general terms (the characteristic working *milieu*) and, in the narrow sense of a particular group's changing task upon the shape of the leadership he is to exercise in contrast to the patterns appropriate in industry, for example. The officer cadet should have a much clearer understanding of the ways in which military leadership is 'like' and 'unlike' other forms of it.

2. *Instructor's Rôle.* This is not markedly different from that in Session 1. The instructor, however, should be able to deploy his professional knowledge and experience with more effect in this session.

3. *Evaluation.* Although this session suffers from juxta-position to the more unusual and 'practical' Session 2, it clearly makes a useful contribution to the course as a whole.

Session 4. 'Twelve O'Clock High'

Description

This consists of another observation exercise, but this time using a film with an armed forces background to provide the 'data'. The film shown—*Twelve O'Clock High*—is a story of an U.S. Air Force bomber group in the Second World War, which is successively led by two leaders. [See Appendix C.] After the first is relieved of his command the film is stopped, and the officer cadets have a chance to discuss in terms of functional leadership why he has failed, and what they would do if they were going to take command of the group. The film then continues with the arrival of the second leader, played by Gregory Peck, and narrates his attempts to raise the morale of the squadrons in his charge. At a suitable point the film is stopped, and the rest of the time is spent in discussing the functions performed by the new leader.

Comments

1. *General.* Besides providing a more relaxed and informal session suitable for the evening, this film observation exercise further enables the officer cadet to see for himself, albeit in a fictional form, a vivid illustration of the general theory of the course. Although the film includes unfamiliar American Air Force jargon and customs, and does not always show to the best advantage due to its date (1950) the fact that it was originally made for entertainment purposes rather than for leadership training enhances its value.

Lastly, it should be stressed that the object of this session is not to contrast a 'bad' with a 'good' leader, but to give students an extended observation exercise in which they can compare the successes and failures of *both* leaders in response to a common problem, making use of an extended range of data which only a film could provide.

2. *Instructor's Role.* The quality of the mid- and post-film discussion depends much upon the skill of the instructor and the standards he has already set and maintained during the course. But the impact of the session as a whole is not completely dependent on him, and it gives the student who may have missed the point of the functional approach so far, to have a fresh look at it in the context of seeing a film. It is therefore to some extent a 'safety net' session.

3. *Evaluation.* Although some officer cadets are 'put off' by the background, quality, or necessarily fictional nature of the film, a substantial majority find this a most valuable exercise, and for some it is the 'highlight' of the course.

Session 5. 'Exercise Remake'

Description

After a night's sleep the students re-assemble in order to tackle a 'case study'. Each is given a written account of a peacetime situation in a unit which is suffering from low morale. The officer cadets are required to discuss the case in their syndicates, diagnosing the deeper causes of the *malaise* and treating those rather than the symptoms. Then in plenary session a representative from each syndicate takes part in a playlet, assuming the role of a second lieutenant at a meeting of officers called to discuss the serious morale situation. In this small drama the 'company commander' would be played by an experienced officer who had not been present previously at the course. Physically, this phase of the session will look like this :

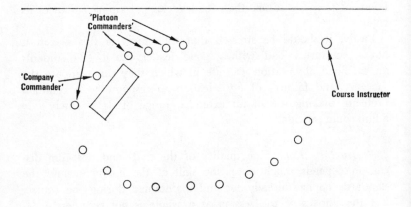

3. LEADERSHIP CASE STUDY PLAYLET

When the 'platoon commanders' have made their points, and these have been accepted or rejected by the 'company commander', the instructor will break off the playlet and initiate some questioning of the actors on their own reactions to the arguments expressed. He will then restore the half circle for the normal plenary phase, and open the discussion along the most promising lines.

Comments

1. *General.* The case study method is valuable because it again allows the student to scrutinise data, diagnose causes and make decisions upon the appropriate remedies. They provide a kind of 'leadership exercise without troops'. Real situations, i.e. ones that have actually happened, are to be used if possible, and they must be of a type that does not demand more technical knowledge than the student possesses. Again, it does not matter too much whether the 'right' solution has been achieved—in most cases there are several equally correct ones, and anyway the student will lack the necessary experience to arrive at more than an out-line answer. What is important, however, is the way the problem is approached, and (in the context of the course) whether the students are putting their recently acquired knowledge of func-tional leadership to good use.

2. *Instructor's Role.* The session is usually enjoyed by instructor and officer cadets alike, and it is not difficult to lead. The case-study sparks off plenty of discussion, and the instructor may guide this to some extent by the carefully timed question of observation. At this stage he may also be able to speak from his own experience of regimental life with much greater effect than if he had done so during the early part of the course.

3. *Evaluation.* On average, the 'case study' session is usually rated high by the officer cadets. This may, in part, be due to a natural rise in interest as the course nears its end, coupled with the fact that after a night's sleep, minds are fresh. But the 'practical' approach of dealing with a concrete problem, and the introduc-tion to a decision-making role, make this a most effective session.

Session 6. Course Summary

Description

This session resembles the first one in arrangement. For syndicate discussion three questions are pinned up on sheets of paper :

What have you learnt on this course?

What do you still need to know more about?

How can you apply what you have learnt?

For the sake of time, each syndicate is restricted to reporting three answers to each question. At the end of 45 minutes, the instructor receives and writes up the four reports, and initiates the closing discussion.

Comments

1. *General.* The purpose of this session is to build on the process which has already begun in the students' mind of relating prospectively the theory of leadership to practical experience of his next steps in his Army career, namely his senior terms at Sandhurst and his years as a platoon or troop commander. In addition, it consolidates what has been already learnt, and opens the way to further instruction.

2. *Instructor's Role.* To a certain extent the instructor on this kind of informal and concentrated educational course may be compared to the pilot of a jet airliner. He must work hard to get the aircraft off the ground, and then he can sit back while the 'automatic pilot' flies the plane. But the landing once more demands all his skill and training. So the instructor must be able to 'earth' the insights gained on the course so that the students not only break up as a group with the feeling that they have not been wasting their time, but also with the positive sense that what they have learnt is relevant to them both in understanding more clearly the leadership of others, and in discharging their own duties as leaders more effectively.

3. *Evaluation of Whole Course.* After the sixth and last session the students are asked to evaluate the course as a whole. The cadets are also asked in this final reaction sheet to suggest improvements to the course, and to make any other comments they like about it.

Summary

Such a concentrated course as that described above cannot *teach* leadership : it can only provide opportunities for the students to *learn* for themselves. Thus there is an important 'take it or leave it' element in the course : in this field the 'sacred right of rejection' has to be guarded at all costs. Therefore it is not a sign of failure if a proportion of students do not accept the functional approach to leadership either as a rough statement of the truth or as a theory which may inform their practice. Here it is important to recollect one of the primary purposes of such a course, which is to induce the student to think for himself about a vital element of his job. We may create the conditions in which he can do this, but we cannot engineer his conclusions. Divergence of views and the independent mind which is critical of what appears to be a majority opinion are to be welcomed rather than tolerated, for unless we are at liberty to disagree there is no real freedom to agree.

On the other hand, nothing is served by a feigned agnosticism on the part of the instructor. Unless he is convinced both by reason and experience that the general theory which forms the core of the course is closer to the truth than any other available concept, he will not be able to explain it with much conviction. It will be 'someone else's theory', not something which he has seen and understood for himself. Granted he does know what he is talking about, the instructor has to avoid the temptation of a 'frontal assault' upon the minds of his hearers behind a barrage of his own enthusiasm. Such behaviour only arouses opposition and defeats its own end. A strategy of the 'indirect approach', however, which does not make the acceptance of any doctrine the explicit aim, avoids that obvious pitfall and incidentally provides the best guarantee that the functional approach will be given a fair hearing.

Such considerations make it a difficult matter to decide the degree of success or failure of such courses. Yet leadership training, like any other form of education, bears a price tag. This can be calculated in two main categories: time and money. Clearly the allocation of even a small proportion of student and instructor time (and the corresponding share of the taxpayers' or firm's money) will depend upon the judgments of those in responsible positions concerning the merits of the actual, or proposed, training. Some form of such cost accounting in education is unavoidable. In addition, those who have direct responsibility for such a course need some yardstick to assess its effectiveness, i.e. the extent to which the methods of education employed fulfil the aims of the leadership syllabus, otherwise they are working in the dark when they attempt to improve it. Therefore, the criteria upon which a course will be judged have to be carefully worked out.

In the case of a concentrated leadership course, there seem to be four possible criteria which, when combined can give a reasonably accurate reading on the success, or failure meter.

1. *Student reaction.* Both the written and verbal reactions of the

student to the course provide some evidence of how much he has thought and learnt for himself. And in such a subject as leadership, the reception by the student of what is heard and seen is a vital factor. If there is a strong negative response in either his rating or his comments it is unlikely that he has gained much from the course. Conversely, a strong measure of interest suggests that in some ways the course has fulfilled its purposes.

Since 1964 until the date of publication some 3,000 officer cadets at the Royal Military Academy have taken part in the functional leadership training course outlined in this chapter. Beginning with the Royal Air Force College at Cranwell in 1965, a number of other officer training schools have studied and adopted the Sandhurst approach. The include the Officer Cadet Training Unit at R.A.F. Henlow, the Royal Military Academy of the Norwegian Army, the Women's Royal Army Corps College, the Aircrew Officer's Training School at R.A.F. Fenton, and the Royal Navy Special Duties Officers' School at Portsmouth. Consequently the total of those who have evaluated the course since its inception is now over 8,000 men and women. Each has evaluated every session, and the whole course. On the percentage scale, the average rating at Sandhurst has been calculated at 70 per cent (between 'Good' and 'Very Good'). On the nine-point scale used in the Royal Air Force (and now at Sandhurst) the average over-all assessment for the first 15 courses at Henlow varied between 6.7 and 8.1, with 12 ratings between 7.0 and 7.5.

The Henlow findings are particularly interesting because the O.C.T.U. range of cadets—graduates and professionally qualified, mature technical men, young men and women—is probably nearest to the range of executive entrants to industry and commerce. Thus the course has also proved its worth in the training of the older Non-Commissioned Officers who have been selected for commissions. It is also being effectively used for developing leadership at 'supervisor' and 'foreman' level. For example, the No. 1 Air Electronics School, R.A.F. Topcliffe, where N.C.O. air electronics aircrew are trained, has also been using the functional leadership course since early 1967.

2. *Student performance.* It is natural for people to show a high degree of interest after an unusual course which has stimulated their thought and exposed them to new ideas. But the novelty may wear off, and the enthusiasm, though genuine at the time, prove to be transitory. An important complementary criterion

is therefore the extent to which those students who accept the functional approach to leadership as a useful concept actually apply it subsequently, either to analyse other leaders, or in their own practice. This can barely be measured; we can only be aware whether or not it is happening. [See Appendix D.]

3. *Instructor reaction.* The informed opinion of the instructors, who possess direct experience of the kind of situations the students will be required to perform in as leaders, is clearly valuable. Whether they believe the course is effective or not is therefore evidence that must be taken into serious account.

4. *Consultant opinion.* The fourth criteria is the judgment or opinion of outside specialists in the field of leadership training. These can act as consultants bringing their wider experience of the way principles are translated into practice to bear upon the problems of assessing a course in terms of effectiveness.

From these four yardsticks a composite impression may be formed which possesses some validity, and it would be unwise to neglect any of them. We are standing on the threshold of new developments in leadership training, and only an accurate and objective evaluation of present methods can point the way forward.

CHAPTER SIX

FIELD LEADERSHIP TRAINING

The principle of field leadership training is a simple one, namely that the student should be given a rôle as a leader of a group operating in the 'characteristic working situation' of the organisation. In practice most organisations will find it impossible to create that 'characteristic working situation' with authenticity, and so a compromise may have to be accepted. Given the practical training opportunities, there remains the educational problem of exploiting it to the best advantage. In order to show how this task can be approached I shall again give a concrete example— the leadership training of officer cadets at Sandhurst.

The officer cadet spends a considerable amount of his time on field exercises designed to extend his tactical knowledge and such technical skills as wireless operating and map reading. On many of these occasions individuals have the chance of acting as platoon commanders, sergeants or section leaders. This practice in command appointments reaches a climax for the senior intake during a second spell of overseas training, which takes place only a few weeks before their commissioning ceremony.

Although the primary purpose of overseas training is to give the officer cadet some tactical experience at platoon and company level, it is likely that even without any explicit mention of the subject, some valuable lessons will be learnt about leadership. This judgment is borne out by the 1962 questionnaire already mentioned, which was given to 142 senior officer cadets who had just returned from two weeks of field training in Cyprus, training in which instructor comment had been confined largely to tactical performance. The replies to the question—'Assess the Winter Overseas Training from the point of view of how much you have learnt about leadership'—established that 64 per cent of those asked had found the exercises of 'good value' or 'some value'. Thus the natural grouping of the officer cadets to practise tactical manoeuvres brought with it a marked degree of leadership development. Therefore, as so often in education, it was not a question of making a clean sweep and starting again, but of grafting on to a living stem new ideas which would, to change the metaphor, increase the yield of the crops per acre.

How could this be done? Not unnaturally I looked first to see whether any other armed forces were tackling the same problem of marrying up a broadly functional approach to leadership with practical field exercises extending over a reasonable period of time. In 1961 a paper entitled 'Leadership in Small Military Units: Some Recent Research Findings' by Dr Carl J. Lange, was read at a N.A.T.O. symposium. This gave in outline the researches of the U.S. Army Infantry Human Research Unit (Fort Benning, Georgia) in conjunction with the George Washington University Human Resources Research Office towards answering the question 'How does the leader function to maintain high motivation and high standards of performance among his followers?'

Although the Americans at Fort Benning were slowly evolving their own functional leadership training programme this did not include the inter-relation of theory and practical experience in the way I envisaged. More hopeful were the remarks of M. Lhotellier after Dr Lange's paper :

It is in this field of applied research that the psychologist can demonstrate the validity of his work even to those military users who know least about it. It is important to conduct experiments with a common methodology; experiments to shed light upon methods of leadership and reactions to leadership in the different countries.

This is what I am trying to do at the Inter-Arm Military School at St Cyr at Coetquidan, while teaching social psychology in the Faculty of Letters and Human Sciences at Rennes University. After a first stage of training by the group dynamics method I intend next year to extend the training to exercises on the ground, with the necessary control by military experts. To this end the preparation of filmed case-studies with the help of I.S.H.A. (The Institute of Applied Human Sciences) will be a valuable aid; and all these exercises will complete a comprehensive theoretical course in military psycho-sociology.

Interested by this proposal to develop field leadership training in the French Army I visited St Cyr in 1963 only to find that M. Lhotellier's place had been taken by another social psychologist from the same University and that nothing had come from these promising remarks.

Another attempt to train leaders in the field at that time merits attention. For some years the Royal Air Force College at Cranwell sent its senior officer cadets on a 'Leadership Training Camp' in Cyprus. Working in small groups the cadets were given tough physical tasks to perform, involving several days of hard living in the mountains. Two points may be made about such camps. First, leadership training could be called a symbiotic activity, i.e. it flourishes best alongside other forms of training. [Symbiosis, a biological term, is defined as 'permanent union between organisms each of which depends for its existence on the other' (*Concise Oxford Dictionary*)]. When isolated and made the centre of educational programmes it often shows signs of malnutrition. Secondly, the instructors attached to each group possessed at that time only a list of ten qualities which they used to rate each cadet's leadership. In other words, the emphasis remained still on *assessment*. Since 1963 both these defects have been remedied.

In summary, therefore, it may be said that there had been no serious attempt to apply the concept of functional leadership to the problem of field leadership training in the military sphere prior to 1963. Before this date, the old dichotomy between 'theory' and 'practice'—indoors syllabus and outdoor training—reigned supreme. Yet no significant progress could be made until this partition had been broken down in the minds of instructors and students. Without models from other armies, parts of the armed forces, or industry, it was necessary at Sandhurst to initiate our own experiments in this vital area.

In the summer of 1965 for the first time both the senior and junior intakes going on overseas training had passed through the concentrated functional leadership course—some months before in the case of the former, and six weeks in that of the latter. Now they would be living and working together for ten days among the wooded hills of the Eiffel region of South Germany. The objective of research from the leadership point of view was a limited one, namely to discover whether the officer cadets had made the functional approach their own, and how far they found it useful as an aid to observe and interpret the examples of others.

In order to find out this information each officer cadet was asked to complete a questionnaire at the end of the training period. At the top he gave his company, intake and command appointment (if any), but not his name. The questions, spaced out on foolscap, were as follows :

1. What have you chiefly learnt about leadership during this period of Overseas Training?
2. Give one example of a function meeting task, team maintenance and individual needs which you have observed in the field.
3. Any other comments?

The responses made by 420 officer cadets under these headings defy close categorisation. There were, however, a number of common observations. In particular many commented upon the effects of stress upon leadership. Besides the pressures of completing tasks against the clock, and travelling over long stretches of rough country, the officer cadets in command appointments had to deal with the effects of almost continuous cold rain upon platoon and section morale. Thus some seniors said that they had learnt :

That when everyone gets tired it is up to those in command to maintain the standard and to set an example. That encouragement goes a long way with tired men, but will not always be enough. A certain amount of pressure must be maintained. Tired men will instinctively obey a forceful command from a forceful commander.

Fitness and endurance are needed in a leader, so that he is able to think clearly under stress and act quickly although tired.

The greater the stress the more attention must be given to functional leadership. Under normal conditions it is possible to get away with 'drill book' leadership.

The commander must never show himself to be 'pushed' or worried by any physical or mental situation in which he finds himself.

Some seniors also experienced the extra resources which the

responsibility of command releases in the leader, noting :

That if you hold a command appointment it is much easier to go on when you are really tired.

While holding a command appointment one completely forgets and overcomes tiredness (physical and mental), and one's only concern becomes the completing of the task and the welfare of the men.

Self must come last. Having a command appointment gives one extra reserves of energy. One can go on with food for that extra hour whilst the platoon feeds.

Another series of comments referred to the commander's need to delegate authority to sub-commanders and to work through them in order to achieve the task assigned to him. Thus some said that they had learnt :

How to delegate, i.e. not to rush around doing everything, but to give subordinates responsible tasks and simply to supervise.

How difficult it is to lead unless one has full support from the platoon sergeant and section commanders, and they in turn get support from their men.

To lead you don't have to do everything. Leave platoon sergeant and section commanders to do their own jobs.

A number of the junior intake, who served on overseas training as the riflemen in the platoons commanded by seniors, had clearly observed the leadership of the seniors and learnt some valuable lessons :

Under a certain amount of strain it is difficult to put leadership into practice. Being in the junior intake I saw leadership from the 'receiving' end. Of those given appointments, I much preferred to be led by some rather than others, and the difference particularly struck me. By personality some could get even 'dirty' jobs done easily, while others who 'put one's back up' would have to go to great lengths.

In the second phase the individual was forgotten, as leaders felt the strain themselves and were not conscious of others...

The difficulty of meeting the three areas of need. Most of our commanders were too occupied with the task in hand to worry about team maintenance and individual needs. Consequently we were, at times, left in the dark as to what we were meant to be doing, due to insufficient briefing.

Tiredness can affect one greatly. A person can completely change when tired. Also, people very soon notice when the leader is thinking of himself first.

We were given the opportunity to see how our seniors commanded men. During the two weeks I was able to see how different seniors set about the same job, and learn which was the most successful way. I have learnt to be critical of the methods adopted by leaders.

By watching those who had been given appointments I learnt that one had to lead by example. It was almost easier to say that I learnt more about how not to be a leader than how to be one—from their mistakes.

On Saturday, 10th July, we had just completed a long and miserable night in defence, yet the section was in fairly good spirits. However, a change in appointments took place. The new section commander had one very simple task—to get his section washed, shaved, fed and ready to move off in an hour. In five minutes he succeeded in getting everyone's back up. Not only did he fail in his task, he also ruined a team and had no regard for individual need. This was brought out not only by his treatment of people in his section, but also by his own too obvious careless attitude to the whole thing.

In contrast, a patrol leader who took us on a four-hour patrol in terrible weather conditions, who succeeded in getting lost five times, achieved completely different results. Because he was vitally interested in what he had to do, and communicated this interest to others in his patrol, we returned exhausted but in extremely good spirits. After a short rest we set out on an ambush with the rest of the platoon in much better shape than those who had remained behind the whole afternoon.

Our Directing Staff sergeant almost personified leadership if the three areas of need are a quick definition of leadership task. He kept morale high throughout. Made tea for late night patrols in the most adverse conditions, treated each man as an individual, catering for their needs whether medical or nutritional.

Still more observations supported the belief that a leader who is firm and quiet can be more effective than one who is over-vocal and domineering. This is true even in situations of considerable stress :

How quiet confidence and real knowledge of the subject is more effective in leading soldiers than drill square-type bluff.

That contrary to expectation leading can be done in a quiet, civilised, cordial manner, provided that the leader has the co-operation and the confidence of the led.

The folly of leading by criticism and shouting. A word of encouragement can be more efficacious.

Principally that outwardly quiet and unassuming people can sometimes make very effective leaders where apparently effective characters have failed.

Too often clumsy rebukes do more harm than good.

The best leaders were seldom ones with the loudest voices.

The demagogic personality is not good—a quieter approach to leading is far more of a success, dealing in turn with the areas of need in a methodical—not mechanical—way. The brash 'Follow me!' or 'O.K?' after every order is not effective, not natural, and easily imitated. A quiet unassuming leader is noticed only by his silent efficiency . . . Leadership is motivated by self-sacrifice, and not by lowering standards to the general level.

The bombastic leader never gets results. T.I.M. is not theoretical nonsense but practical and necessary. [T.I.M. is an abbreviation for Task, Individual Needs and (Team) Maintenance.]

Closely related to this perception that a particular style of command is likely to be more effective than others was an appreciation of the importance of example in leadership :

The most powerful way to lead is by example.

Leadership *is* example.

One must set an example. I noticed that if I tried to do my best others followed—and vice versa.

Team spirit is instilled by good example and good organisation by commanders.

A large number of both senior and junior officer cadets showed an appreciation of the effects of task performance on morale. In this connection they became aware of which leadership functions were either poorly done or omitted altogether, often with marked impact upon team maintenance. Perhaps the leadership function most commonly singled out for comment was the 'briefing'. This is a key function, for unless the team members know what the task is, they cannot participate very fully. Moreover, a leader must 'relate the group emotionally to the task'; he must explain if possible, not only *what* is to be done, but *why* it is necessary and important; how it fits into the wider pattern of the main plan. In other words, although the task does not arise in the group, but is given to it from above, the leader must ensure as far as possible that it becomes *their* task. In fact, working groups in any sort of organisation welcome this kind of 'briefing' and many show signs of the lack of it in the areas of team maintenance and individual needs, if it is not given. Cadet comments support these conclusions :

The understanding of tasks by the troops throughout the second phase was often totally lacking. This was due to very bad handing down of orders—especially on the cordon of the village, where I, and I think everyone else, had almost no notion as to what was happening.

The correct use of good clear orders has not been appreciated by many cadets.

Before one can lead, the followers must know their task.

We, as riflemen, were rarely given a good 'aim'. It is most important that the private soldier knows *exactly* (where possible) what he is going to do, and what task both he and his sub-unit is to fulfil.

Only a sketchy outline of imminent parts of a phase were given, and hence interest in an exercise was lost.

In a command appointment one can get anything done willingly as long as the men know why they have been asked to do it.

In defence, my section commander gave his orders well. It is not sufficient to rattle off orders... It is more important to ensure that the men know what is going on and what is expected of them. In this case, my unit commander was able to give feeling to his orders, so that the section became aware of its responsibilities. I knew how my arcs of fire overlapped those of adjoining trenches, and now the sector was mutually supporting. Morale was thus high.

But there are many other task functions which the platoon commander must master. Map-reading, for example, is the skill by which an officer leads his men to their objective. If he cannot read a map, the group will not achieve its task, and team maintenance will suffer :

We were misled occasionally due to bad map-reading—a most demoralising experience. Therefore the leader must be absolutely sure of his map reading.

Good leadership can only come from a thorough knowledge of one's job. The latter was made more than clear after seeing the mistakes which resulted from both lack of knowledge and lack of confidence.

On the other hand, the successful completion of the unit's task will have some noticeable effects on 'group cohesiveness' and morale :

On this particular fighting patrol it was (needless to say) pouring with rain and soon everyone was soaked through, cold and despondent. However, by encouragement, pushing, and a certain 'amount of luck, a very successful action was fought. The effect on the fighting patrol was extraordinary. Once more they felt themselves to be a closely knit unit.

The successful leader, however, was not only competent in performing his tasks, he could also hold his team together. In this respect many officer cadets recognised the importance of justice in the allocation of duties. On the whole, members of platoons did not resent onerous duties, or lack of food and sleep, providing they were necessary, but they reacted against unnecessary hardship resulting from either conditions which could be improved, or the unfair allocation of work. Thus, justice must not only be done, but it must also be seen to be done :

One thing stands out. In order to lead any sort of unit it is necessary to be absolutely fair in everything—sharing of extra duties, extra loads, food etc. If this is not so, those under you lose all respect rapidly.

The best example of team maintenance was the organisation of a roster involving feeding and sentry duty. Some commanders had no set plan, while others ensured that all did a fair share of the work, and had ample food and rest.

Once one person is isolated as a scapegoat, life deteriorates for the remainder.

Humour also was found to be valuable in conditions of stress and strain, to relieve accumulated tensions :

Towards the end of the second phase morale was low one

morning, and we were tired and wet. Suddenly the Directing Staff Sergeant started to crack jokes, so restoring everyone's morale.

That sense of humour is essential to a leader, and, as strain increases, he becomes lost without one.

The meeting of 'individual needs', so that platoon members could continue to contribute effectively to the common task, occasioned another spate of comments, some directed at the importance of catering for physical needs, and some pointing towards the less tangible ones :

Each patrol was provided with hot drinks no matter what the time. Particularly valuable when all members were wet through. This meant a maintenance of morale and a disregard for the effects of the weather.

Individual needs on the whole were treated rather as a routine —completely worthless.

That in such circumstances it is difficult for a leader to mind individual needs without appearing 'artificial'.

'Using the same two riflemen as scouts in a section throughout a phase, so they knew their job exactly and took a pride in it.

There were many examples of unconscious concern for individual needs by section commanders with a genuine interest in the members of their section. Small things, like a word of praise, a lightening of the load, all helped to boost individual morale.

Leaders must continually look to individual needs of men as well as encourage sections as a whole. Only when a section is well informed and cared for by the leader does it work efficiently.

The importance of giving everyone a task and thus making each person feel he is part of the team effort.

In my section, a rifleman had his 21st birthday. He received no mail and few knew about it. My section commander told me about it and urged me to congratulate him. We all ate together, and cans of beer appeared. Not only was the rifleman happier, but section morale rose. *Individual needs* must be fulfilled to maintain team morale.

One cadet in my section always had difficulty in keeping up; this, I think, was due to his being bored. I therefore gave him the radio—this meant he had to stick close to me, and he got more information than he would otherwise have obtained. Thus, in spite of carrying 10 lb. more, he woke up and found it easier to carry on.

Many officer cadets had found confirmation during overseas training of the functional approach to leadership which they had accepted intellectually on the concentrated course :

Reading through my notes on leadership taken during the course in term 3, I was able to confirm for myself what was mentioned then.

Any commander was able to be criticised under the three headings, and this method seems a good concrete method of identifying an abstract ability—leadership.

The difficulty of practising the theory of leadership. It is always easier to take an example after it has happened and analyse it in terms of task, individual and team maintenance, but much harder to apply the principles before or during a command appointment.

I have learnt a lot about leadership during this period of overseas training, but the most important lesson is that any leader must fulfil these three things—Task, Team Maintenance and Individual Need—if he wants to be successful in his object.

Lastly, a significant percentage expressed the desire for a more, or better leadership training—a healthy sign :

Next year I shall find it much easier to be a commander, having seen the seniors this year making successes or failures.

We only had one discussion of leadership in the field—could this not be increased?

A brief revision period on the theoretical side of 'leadership', i.e. the three circles, before overseas training would have been of beneficial value.

Perhaps a smaller gap between the initial leadership training and the practice period of overseas training would have produced even better results.

Many of our commanders, who seemingly had a good grip on the situation when not 'pressed' in any way, tended to forget very basic points when under more trying conditions. The theory of leadership that is learnt at the R.M.A. does not go deep enough into the problem of the application of what we have learnt when we are not sitting in a comfortable chair in the company anteroom.

*   *   *

As a result of the experiment in the summer of 1965, certain decisions were made with reference to the next spell of overseas training, which would take place in Libya in December of the same year. These may be listed as follows :

1. to give both the senior and junior intakes a 'refresher' period of discussion on the general theory of group needs and functional leadership shortly before they went abroad.
2. to brief the 12 captains who would be acting as Directing Staff instructors upon the leadership training aspect of their role.
3. to set aside an hour in the mid-training break for a discussion by officer cadets of the leadership displayed in the first phase.
4. to continue the experiment of issuing reaction sheets at the end, both for research and educational reasons.

Conditions in Libya were much better than those in Germany six months earlier. Fair weather and a less hectic programme enabled tactical lessons to be learnt more thoroughly, but lowered the strain upon leaders. Consequently there were fewer vivid examples of team maintenance functions. In most cases the smooth performance of the set tasks sufficiently raised morale without any deliberate effort by the leader. Task functions, such as briefing and map reading, seem to have been done with efficiency. Yet most, if not all, of the 'chief lessons' learnt in Germany, such as the importance of the leader's own example, and the equitable distribution of duties or chores, emerged again in a muted form.

When asked how far the officer cadets in their platoons had been aware of the functional approach to leadership given to them in the concentrated course, the Directing Staff instructors replied in the following vein :

Cadets were well aware of the 'leadership circles' and had a fairly lengthy discussion on the subject during the pre-overseas training exercise. I noticed in particular that commanders worked hard to create the right atmosphere and to meet individual needs.

Awareness from the junior intake was good, and observations were offered freely. The seniors needed more prompting, and were less willing to point out functions left out or badly done by their fellows.

In the final discussion, all thought they had learnt a lot about leadership, and I was interested to see that the juniors had cottoned on to the fact that the 'team maintenance ball' doesn't need much oiling when things are going well, which (unfortunately?) they did most of the time.

Considerable extent : evident by comments referring to the relevant parts of the course as incidents occurred. Both negative and positive aspects were noted; thus seniors criticised each other in terms of functions when they failed in leadership— and were equally quick to praise leadership actions which obviously resulted in benefit to the platoon.

It is difficult to assess how much is due to innate leadership ability, and how much to leadership training. However, from cadets' performances in command appointments, and their comments on the performance of others, it is obvious that the main points put over during the one day course are remembered and applied.

The senior intake, in particular, showed considerable awareness of the functional approach to leadership. They constructively criticised leadership deficiencies among themselves, and also one or two examples from the platoon and company directing staff. The juniors appeared less aware of the approach, even though they had more recently completed the course.

A considerable amount by both intakes. I had briefed them to think in terms of the 'three circles', and most note-books had them at the top of the page to remind them early on. However, this reminder was not necessary in the last phase, and where one of the three needs failed to be met, the cadet concerned was usually aware of it, and admitted so in his self-critique at the end of a command appointment.

These comments reveal, as another officer put it, that both the staff and the cadets were beginning to speak a common language in their discussion of leadership, one which was more adequate to the subject than that of traits and qualities. Inevitably, in the early stages of a very slow and gradual process of change, there were varying degrees of fluency in that language, which in turn, to some extent reflected different levels of understanding. But at least a start had been made, a basis for further experiment.

Certainly the periods of overseas exercises since Libya in 1965 involving over 2,000 cadets, have marked a steady growth in the effectiveness of field leadership training. In particular the Directing Staff captains, briefed on this aspect of their role within their first week of joining Sandhurst, have become more adept at commenting on leadership in tactical situations. The essential principle of leadership training, that theory should be related to practice, seems to have been more than confirmed.

In discussing the results or effects of leadership training, it is perhaps important not to compare the top 10 per cent of leaders who command naturally with the more 'average' who, newly conscious of the requirements of leadership, deliberately set about supplying the necessary functions. Officer cadets, understandably, prefer the natural leader, little realising that often this kind of ability can become either fixed at a certain level or ceiling, or become rigid and stiff with advancing age and changing circumstances. In fact, leaders on all points of the continuum of leadership ability in order to grow have to pass through a period of 'artificiality' or self-consciousness, as they awkwardly apply theory to practice, or reflect upon their experience in new terms. Learning to drive a car, to use steering wheel, gear lever and foot pedals at the same time, plunges us into a number of uncomfortable stages before it becomes second nature, and we are scarcely conscious of the combinations. One officer cadet perceived the process of leadership training in a similar light :

The three circles ... are of no possible use if thought of consciously. It would be absurd to stop in the middle of an action and think of them as such. They must link up with our inherent leadership in the subconscious mind and discipline it so that the Aim, Team Maintenance and Individual Needs become the natural channels through which we can lead our units.

Because of this need for a disciplined, although not stereotyped, leadership, we must be taught these principles while at Sandhurst and—until they come to us without our having to think about the three circles, we must continually and consciously consider these circles in everything that has any flavour of leadership about it ... If they only have to be used occasionally instead of persistently, they will never become subconscious.

*　　*　　*

Much of this chapter has been concerned with the final leadership training given to the senior intake in the summer of 1965. Within two weeks of returning from Germany, these officer cadets were commissioned, and 'passed out' at a Sovereign's Parade taken in person by Her Majesty the Queen. There is perhaps no more fitting way to conclude these three chapters on leadership training at the Royal Military Academy Sandhurst than to quote Her Majesty's address to the Senior Division, which perfectly sums up the nature and responsibilities of military leadership :

Today, those of you in the Senior Division become officers and it will not be long before those in the other Divisions follow in your steps. The day on which you receive your Commission is one of the most important in your life, because your duties and responsibilities as leaders of men are among the most onerous your country can confer upon you.

You have learnt here that an officer must be, above all else, a leader; a person whom men will follow into danger, discomfort and every ordeal which nature, climate or a human enemy can contrive. Remember always that the best and purest form of leadership is example; that 'Come on' is a much better command than 'Go on'.

You come of races renowned for courage and I know that as officers you will never fail to be the first in danger. But leadership in the stress and excitement of battle will not be your only responsibility. Your patience, inspiration and attention to detail will also be required in the often equally testing routine duties and in what may seem uneventful and even unimportant periods of service. These times call for leadership of a special kind if you are to keep the morale and efficiency of your men at the pitch required.

Leadership demands a dedicated responsibility towards the men under your command. Their lives will be in your hands and they will have the right to expect from you the highest standards of character, professional competence and integrity. If you will always put their interests and welfare before your own, you will not fail them and together you will be able to undertake any enterprise.

You will often inspect your men, I suspect that when you are doing so they will be just as keenly inspecting you.

Soldiers have always been ambassadors and representatives of their country. This applies with even greater force to officers. Your civilian countrymen will—perhaps unconsciously—pay you the compliment of expecting you to show, not only a higher degree of courage and duty than themselves, but, when serving abroad, a standard of behaviour which reflects well upon your country.

As you join your Units, you will be stepping into a profession which has played a most important and distinguished part in the evolution of this country. I am confident that you will continue to uphold its tradition as servant and protector of the state.

The path on which you are now setting out will often be rough and steep; my trust, my thoughts and my good wishes go with you on it.

CHAPTER SEVEN

DEVELOPING LEADERSHIP IN INDUSTRY

Leadership and Management

'In industry we are frequently faced, though rarely in such specific terms as in the Services, with the problem of defining what we mean by leadership, and why we need it.' So wrote the training manager of a large firm in a letter to the author. "Although industry," he added in a subsequent conversation, "has tended to shy away from the word 'leadership' the reality behind it has now come to be recognised as an ingredient in successful managers. Can it be developed?" In different words many other managers have made the same point and asked the same question of the author, especially in the past two years as large numbers of industrial firms, commercial enterprises and public service organisations have heard about the experimental leadership training in the armed services. Can the methods of developing leadership potential accepted and proved in the Services, be applied to the training of managers?

Before answering this question however, it is necessary to raise a further one : 'To what extent and in what ways is the manager a leader?' On the one hand some would want to make a sharp distinction between 'management' and 'leadership' while on the other hand others would virtually equate them. Are the terms inter-changeable?

In reply to these questions the author would refer the reader back to the conclusions of Chapter 1, that essentially leadership lies in the provision of the functions necessary for a group to achieve its task and be held together as a working team. Now this is basic, the raw 'silver' called leadership, which to some extent may be separated and analysed in functional terms. But in reality leadership always appears in a particular form or 'vessel' which can be distinguished from others. This shape is fashioned above all by the *characteristic working situation* of the group or its parent organisation. To some extent the degree of participation in decision-making by group members may be used as a measure to contrast these different forms of leadership, but there are other variables as well. In the military *milieu* the shape which leadership assumes is best called 'Command'; in the industrial and commercial situation it is known as 'Management'. Two boughs from the same trunk, they can easily—but should not be —confused.[1]

In particular the modern industrial situation dictates a necessary technical knowledge for the leader. Besides the particular knowledge required for the firm or branch of business or industry in which he finds himself, the manager should also possess a general technical knowledge of the way in which scientific techniques can be systematically employed for the efficient use of resources. But management techniques do not qualify a man for leadership in industry. They are only effective as extensions of leadership functions. Far from occupying a remote corner in 'industrial sociology' or 'industrial relations', leadership is *the* integrating concept, relating and binding together those subjects which are loosely grouped together as 'Management Studies' in business schools and universities.

'It is the job of leaders in industry, as elsewhere, to get the best—the very best—out of everybody,' said Sir Basil Smallpiece, chairman of Cunard, in a lecture to the Institute of Directors reported in *The Times* (11 Nov. 1966). 'This needs two things. First, to see that everyone fully understands the purpose of the new thinking, that they appreciate the policy needed for the business to prosper, and how this will affect people and their jobs. This is why I have been meeting Cunard's staff in our ships, to see that every man jack of them understands what we are up against.

'And secondly, it is the task of leaders so to organize the business that the people in it can work freely and effectively together. In these ways, untold resources of new energy will be released at all levels of a company. And so it should be surely, with our national affairs.'

Some managers assume that leadership is 'easier' in the armed services than in industry. 'We have no Queen's Regulations,' lamented one. But this is an unrealistic assessment. In fact there are advantages and disadvantages as far as leadership is concerned in both fields. For example, the serviceman rarely sees an 'end product' to his labours; it is often difficult for him to regard his tasks in tangible, worthwhile or profitable terms, a factor which may contribute to a lack of enthusiasm on the job.

One important and obvious difference between the general leadership situations of industry and Armed Forces (in the United Kingdom and America, but not—for example—in Germany or Norway) is the existence of trades unions in the former. They provide a 'third dimension' in industrial relations which render many comparisons between the Services and industry invalid.

Within the terms of this book the Trades Union movement could be understood in the following way. Although the three areas of *task, team maintenance* and *individual needs* overlap and can mutually influence each other for good (see pp. 15–18) it is also possible that the circles could be pulled out so that they no longer touch. In other words, the most effective pursuit of the group's 'task' can come into conflict with the satisfaction of some or all of the 'individual needs' of its members. The Trades Unions may be seen as bodies organised to protect and promote the 'individual needs' circle, in the context of—or over against if need be—the task and team maintenance of the organisation.

For historical, social and psychological reasons a degree of tension, and some would say potential—but not necessarily open—conflict, is unavoidable between the 'task' and the 'individual' areas of need in industry as in any other large organisation. This potential conflict of interests forms a challenge to the 'team maintenance' abilities of industrial and commercial leadership. And the way of meeting it lies in ensuring that the three areas of need always in fact overlap and are seen to do so. This may involve a redefinition and interpretation of the organisations aims, and a better communication of their true nature.

One manager now responsible for industrial relations in a nationalised industry recently summed up the situation in these words : 'Although it is in the interests of both management and unions that industry should develop and grow, when it comes to deciding how the benefits of growth and development should be shared their interest are not the same, nor will they necessarily agree about the best method of promoting growth. Essentially the rôle of the unions is to look after the interests of their members (in the long term as well as the short term), while management has to judge what is in the best interests of shareholders and customers as well as employees. The fact that their interests are bound to clash when it comes to deciding who gets what share of the cake all too often obscures the point that management and unions need to co-operate together to increase the total size of the cake and must co-operate if the economic objectives of the company and all the people in it are to be achieved.'[2]

If the Trades Unions therefore solve many individual welfare problems for management they can also pose others of a 'team maintenance' nature. Because of them, leadership in industry may encounter different problems and opportunities than in the Services, but it retains its essential nature as the functional response to—or responsibility for—the task, team maintenance and individual needs of the organisation concerned.

Research into Industrial Leadership

Despite a legion of books on leadership in business and industry there has been comparatively little objective research into the leadership content of management. Two reasons may be adduced for this deficiency. Management schools and university departments have tended to shy away from leadership as a rather intangible subject, important but not capable of measurement. Meanwhile social psychologists, on the whole, have retreated from field work into their laboratories.[3] This is a pity because the pioneer research into industrial social psychology was full of promise.

We may summarise such research as there has been by saying that from an initial preoccupation with the welfare of the individual worker in its physical sense—lighting, heating, floor space, time-and-motion study etc.—the industrial psychologists moved on to discover the phenomenon of 'group personality'. This led to a shift of attention from the individual to the group in the factory. It is generally agreed that the research of Elton Mayo in the Hawthorne Works of the General Electric Company in Chicago between 1924 and 1927 marks the watershed in this development. [Elton Mayo was Professor of Industrial Research at the Harvard Graduate School of Business from 1927 to 1947.]

Research by Professor Mayo and his associates continued at Hawthorne and other factories for a number of years, but agreement upon the interpretation of their work is by no means unanimous. For a discussion of these experiments and the conclusions drawn from them the reader can do no better than consult Dr J. A. C. Brown's chapter on 'The Work of Elton Mayo' in his *The Social Psychology of Industry*.[4] Yet the main significance of the work was widely perceived. Professor Mayo summarised it in the following words : 'The ordinary conception of management-worker relations, as existing between company officials on the one hand, and an unspecified number of individuals on the other, is utterly mistaken. Management, in any continuously successful plant, is not related to single workers but always to working groups. In every department that continues to operate, the workers have—whether aware of it or not—formed themselves into a group with appropriate customs, duties, routines, even rituals; and management succeeds (or fails) in proportion as it is accepted without reservation as author and leaders.'[5] It should be noted, however, that although much was learnt in this early research about industrial groups, and the needs present within them, little or no attention was given to the rôle of leaders within them.

On the other hand, many books and articles upon industrial leadership during and after the 1930's concentrated upon the 'functions of management', such as Planning, Organizing, Coordinating, Directing and Controlling. These were apparently not worked out in the light of the group studies mentioned above, and tended to be related exclusively to task work rather than team maintenance or individual needs. Indeed this growing emphasis on management functions, with the implication that technical competence and knowledge are all-important, may be compared in a very broad and general way to the *situational* understanding of leadership described in Chapter 1. Yet without an understanding of the group and the needs present within it, a list of management functions remains somewhat 'in the air' and may degenerate into clichés in the lecture room.

A living and growing subject such as management requires much more research into leadership, its central content. Such as we have, however, certainly confirms the validity of a broadly functional understanding of its nature, although this does not rule out the possibility of significant progress in the future in identifying more clearly the traits of personality which tend to make a man effective as a manager.[6]

The Areas of Leadership Training in Industry

Any firm or organisation which seeks to develop the leadership potential of its employees might perhaps measure itself under the five headings discussed in Chapter 4 and listed here again: *Structure, Leadership Syllabus, Field Leadership Training, Staff Training,* and *Research and advisory Staff.*

The fundamental question concerning the first area is whether or not the shape of the organisation encourages the development of leadership. For example, is control so tight that junior leaders feel that there is no room for the exercise of initiative? Does the climate repress rather than expand latent leadership ability? Is the promotion system such that the right challenge at the right time cause leaders to grow in professional competence and also in self-confidence?

The organisational structure can also make for—or work against —sound leadership. In his lectures the Director of Industrial Society, Mr John Garnett, has offered this counsel to management: 'Look at the organisational chart from the bottom upwards. Ask the question about each person, 'Who is accountable for getting this man to give of his best to his work?' Who is in charge is often clear in an organisation at the top, but very unclear at the bottom. Is he the chargehand? Is he the foreman? Is he the supervisor? Who is it?

'When deciding at what level accountability for performance is to be put, you must reach a decision about how many people one person can be accountable for, if he is to get anywhere near getting them to give of their best to their work. Clearly, if for technical reasons the job is very complicated, it will need fewer people than if it is relatively simple. However, there is a great deal of experience that suggests that you can never be successful if your lowest level leader is accountable for the performance of more than 25 people.'[7]

The two areas—*Staff Training* and *Research and Advisory Staff*—are equally important. 'Staff Training' in this context means primarily the equipping of a small number of managers with the knowledge and skills necessary to organise short courses in leadership for trainee and junior leaders. In addition, a rather large number of middle and senior staff would need to be initiated into the equivalent of the field leadership trainer role; that is, they must have a chance of discussing together how best to give constructive advice to junior leaders in the same language as that which is learnt on the short course. These requirements presuppose a handful of specialists—the *Research and Advisory Staff*—who have a specific responsibility for devising and maintaining the standards of the company's or industrial group's training courses. In any large organisation which cares about the quality of leadership within it, this essential work should not be left to chance, but clearly allocated to an individual or a committee.

Experiments in Industrial Leadership Training

This section will be devoted to describing and assessing some experiments in developing leadership in a formal way in industry. This account will form a background for the following chapter on the application to the industrial situation of the concentrated functional leadership course devised in the Armed Services and outlined above in Chapter 5.

The leadership syllabus in many management and business schools, as has already been noted, does not exist in its own right, but the subject is 'covered' by one or two lectures in a general course such as Industrial Relations or Industrial Sociology. With these lectures *about* leadership we are not concerned here, for although lecturing on leadership is a valid academic activity it is not a very effective form of leadership training. The latter implies some attempt to relate theory to practice. Therefore it involves practical small group work of some kind.

The use of the small group in educational courses relating to leadership may be traced back to an American movement known as *Group Dynamics*.[8] A short account of this approach in its much smaller British manifestations appeared in *The Times* on 3 June 1965 and deserves full quotation :

The causes of Britain's economic malaise are frequently defined. Slightly less frequently remedies are put forward. After roving round the field of blameworthiness—from the Government, to the trade unions, to accountants—the eye is continually drawn back to managers and the management structure. On the remedy count a more flexible system of promotion allowing younger men to get to the top, a new technology oriented generation of management, new business schools to provide a rigorous training to meet management problems, etc., are put forward.

Assuming that management is basically a matter of personal relations—between individuals, within a group, and between groups—a psychological approach to management problems is gradually gaining ground. A movement based on the Tavistock Institute of Human Relations is spreading the fashion for an exercise sometimes known as 'group dynamics'. There are several variations on this theme, but the basic idea is that a group of people taking part in a training scheme, a business course or one of the Tavistock sessions, should explore together their reactions to each other and behaviour within a group.

This approach assumes that every business contact is conducted on two levels—what seems to be said and decided and the unspoken level, of extending empires, maintaining status, emotional and instinctive reactions. Further, it assumes that to understand what is going on at both levels is necessary to steer business affairs properly. These assumptions would be widely accepted. The question is more whether sensitivity to the unspoken level can be improved, and whether by greater understanding of his own reactions and those of his colleagues a man is better fitted to legislate and innovate in his own modest or influential way.

The general method adopted at the Tavistock Institute and by its emulators is to gather together small groups and, without specific direction, allow them to study and discuss as openly as possible their behaviour together. This can be a catalytic experience since it means that a man reveals to himself and others, fears and emotions which otherwise by an unspoken convention are kept to himself. Organisations whose representatives have attended conferences at the institute make a long and impressive list: I.C.I., Unilever, two gas boards, Stewards and Lloyds, Barclays, de Havilland, Esso, the Electricity Council, and the G.P.O. are a few random names.

The technique has been tried out at the Cranfield one-year management course, one of the first British courses run on Harvard-type lines. A week was devoted to group exploration of course members' careers. The experience of these group sessions is generally voted a painful but valuable experience.

I.C.T. has used group dynamics methods in their training courses for systems analysts. These are the new breed of men responsible for designing computer installations. It is a job concentrating on the design and introduction of big innovations in the operating methods of companies installing computers. Innovation is deeply a matter of human relations. It has to be introduced in the face of instinctive fear of taking risks, of losing status and even of redundancy. The group experience is most valuable in helping a man to understand and control these situations.

That business is to a major extent an affair of personal interactions must be accepted as true even if this is not often admitted. The increased awareness of his own problems and instinctive reactions within a group of people is a frightening but most valuable contribution to a man's managerial competence. It give him both a clear knowledge of his own abilities and limitations and of those people with whom he had to deal.

There can be little doubt that Group Dynamics does develop a sensitivity to one's reactions upon others and this may lead to greater self-knowledge. But as a method of leadership training— one of its avowed aims in management education programmes —Group Dynamics in its pure form is open to criticism on at least four counts.

1. In the first place, the so-called leaderless group which forms the basis of the Group Dynamics seminar has no task but to examine its own 'life' periodically. Therefore the *Task* and *Team Maintenance* circles are, so to speak, separated, and exclusive attention given to the latter. This means that a key area of leadership training, the study of the inter-relationship of task and team maintenance—falls outside the scope of the Group Dynamics 'training group'. Without a task the most distinctive characteristic of the work group or team, the necessity for firm leadership from one person, also disappears.

This drawback of Group Dynamics is now becoming more widely recognised, as two quotations will illustrate.

The first is from L. F. Urwick's critical commentary appended to a recent American book full of Group Dynamics assumptions:

If, in the effort to combat obsolete concepts of economics, we try to divorce the study of people from the purposes for which they co-operate, shall we not fall out of the frying pan into the fire? Practical men who are trying to administer groups of their fellow human beings for this purpose or that will not accept this division of the subject. To them it seems academic and unrealistic. The better leaders they are, the more will their minds be concentrated on the common purpose ... The first function of a leader is representation—to represent the purpose of the group he leads both to the outside world and to those collaborating with him.[9]

From the training angle the Group Dynamics approach has also been criticised for the same reason :

The clear limitations of this method stem from its very nature as a group-orientated and not a task-orientated situation. This means that the substantive content of the training is likely to be far removed from the manager's task in his normal job; and hence to be able to focus on one aspect only—that of social sensitivity. Other aspects, such as those of gaining knowledge of, and insight into the tasks involved in managing a business enterprise, must of necessity receive little or no emphasis.[10]

2. Secondly, there are a number of assumptions about leadership intrinsic to Group Dynamics. These are in fact ideas about leadership which are appropriate enough in the isolated setting of the 'group laboratory', but are irrelevant to the actual situation of industry, commerce of the Armed Services. There is indeed a danger that uncritical students at Group Dynamics should go back to their 'back-home' situations and seek to import the Group Dynamics concept of leadership into them.

An illustration of this last point may be drawn from the writings of Douglas McGregor, a former Professor of Psychology at the Massachusetts Institute of Technology and author of the widely influential book *The Human Side of Enterprise*. Professor McGregor became a college president in 1948, and looking back on his experiences, he had come to several new conclusions :

The first is a conviction that has been derived from my personal struggle with the rôle of college president. Before coming to Antioch I had observed and worked with top executives as an adviser in a number of organizations. I thought I knew how they felt about their responsibilities and what led them to behave as they did. I even thought that I could create a rôle for myself that would enable me to avoid some of the difficulties they encountered. I was wrong! It took the direct experience of becoming a line executive, and meeting personally the problems involved, to teach me what no amount of observation of other people could have taught.

I believed, for example, that a leader could operate successfully as a kind of adviser to his organization. I thought I could avoid being a 'boss'. Unconsciously, I suspect, I hoped to duck the unpleasant necessity of making difficult decisions, of taking the responsibility for one course of action among many uncertain alternatives, of making mistakes and taking the consequences. I thought that maybe I could operate so that everyone would like me—that 'good human relations' would eliminate all discord and disagreement.

I could not have been more wrong. It took a couple of years, but I finally began to realize that a leader cannot avoid the exercise of authority any more than he can avoid responsibility for what happens to his organization. In fact, it is a major function of the top executive to take on his own shoulders the responsibility for resolving the uncertainties that are always involved in important decisions. Moreover, since no important decision ever pleases everyone in the organisation, he must also absorb the displeasure, and sometimes severe hostility, of those who would have taken a different course.

A colleague recently summed up what my experience has taught me in these words : 'A good leader must be tough enough to win a fight, but not tough enough to kick a man when he is down.' This notion is not in the least inconsistent with humane, democratic leadership. Good human relations develop out of strength, not of weakness.[11]

Foremost among these assumptions present in Group Dynamic is the idea that leadership functions should be distributed equally among members of the group, i.e. that leadership inheres in the function and not in a person. The group becomes all important, and the appointed leader is reduced to the status of a 'safety net', to provide needed functions if no one else does.[12] Such an approach, of course, could only be applicable in groups without real tasks given to them which have to be achieved in difficult situations.

Perhaps one reason for the popularity of this equation of leadership with the group as a whole lies in its apparent democratic nature. To some minds in particular the Group Dynamics concept of leaders is 'good' leadership (in the moral sense) because it is 'democratic' rather than 'authoritarian'. The American attitude to leadership appears to be ambivalent. At one pole the idea of leadership focused upon one person seems to be an anathema to the democratic ideal; at the other, there is a strong tendency to give much fuller power to elected leaders than in other cultures. The constitutional position of the President is perhaps repeated throughout the culture. Be this as it may, it is important that political presuppositions should not be allowed to form hidden value-judgments in favour of any particular pattern of leadership. Indeed the labelling of various kinds of leadership as 'autocratic' or 'democratic' invites a confusion of mind which rejects—regardless of the situation—any form of leadership exercised by one person. William H. Whyte Jr., a critic of this process in America, has provocatively declared :

Anti-authoritarianism is becoming anti-leadership. In group doctrine the strong personality is viewed with overwhelming suspicion. The co-operative are those who take a stance directly over the keel; the man with ideas—in translation, prejudices—leans to one side or, worse yet, heads for the rudder.[13]

3. A third reason for rejecting Group Dynamics as a universal method of leadership training is that it possesses cultural overtones which make it less palatable in Europe and other continents than in the United States. Group Dynamics is based on the practice of group introspection. On the whole Americans have a much greater interest and tolerance for both personal and social self-analysis than Europeans. Moreover, as providing a setting whereby people can hope to get to terms with each other at some depth, and strive together towards a common awareness, the Group Dynamics movement may be seen as an attempt to meet a social need in America. This may explain its mushroom growth on one side of the Atlantic compared with its relatively slight lodgement outside the United States.[14]

Indeed, a 'training-group' of 16–20 individuals gathered together from all over America and faced with the task of forming a 'culture in microcosm' represents or expresses the unique problem of the United States over the past century : immigrants from all over the world having to start from scratch to enter or build a new society, with its own values, laws and customs. How far the movement is successful, however, even in this social rôle, is doubtful. My own experience as a member of an otherwise all-American group in a National Training Laboratories two-week seminar at Green Lake, Wisconsin; as co-trainer in a mixed British and American group in England; as trainer to an all-British group drawn from the staffs of colleges of education; and as trainer to one composed of 16 bishops drawn from nine different countries meeting in Boston in 1963, certainly confirms in my own mind these tentative conclusions.

4. A fourth reason for hesitation lies in the tendency for the assumptions of group psychotherapy to invade the training scene. In the United Kingdom group psychotherapists have perhaps shown most interest in the Group Dynamics approach, and have used it effectively for treating sick or socially maladjusted people.[15] In leadership training, however, as in selection (see above p. 64 there is a danger that staff drawn from these specialised disciplines may import the preconceptions and methods appropriate to the medical or remedial fields into the work of developing the leadership potential of normal people, often no doubt much to their confusion.[16]

For these reasons—the divorce of *task* and *team maintenance,* the hidden assumptions on leadership, the distinctive American flavour, and the therapeutic overtones—the author does not believe that the future of leadership training lies with Group Dynamics in its pure or barely disguised forms.

It is important to make these critical observations as Group Dynamics still dominates the leadership training scene in the United States, and to a lesser extent Canada, and some earnestly believe that more British universities and management schools than the one or two who have done so already should adopt this approach. Such evaluations as we have on the effects of Group Dynamics training on a man's performance as a leader in industry and other fields certainly does not warrant this enthusiasm. But these conclusions do not mean that individual managers may not profit personally from participation in this sort of exercise. Nor is it to be forgotten that Group Dynamics as a branch of

academic research has made a valuable contribution to our understanding of both the nature of leadership and also the importance
of small group work in leadership development.

Levels in Leadership Training

Before discussing in the following chapter in some detail an
alternative form of leadership training which retains the
advantages and dispenses with the disadvantages of Group
Dynamics, it is important to make a general point, namely that
leadership training can take place on various levels corresponding
to the basic tiers of management. From the standpoint of training
this book on the whole is concerned with the first level, the introduction of the student to the subject. Courses on this level may
perhaps be best given to those who are about to take up their first
main appointment which requires them to act in the role of leader.
There is wide agreements that the lecture as a principal means
of instruction is of limited value at this level, compared with the
use of small group practical work with comment.

In the 'middle management' area one would expect more
emphasis upon the functions of leadership, such as *delegating*
and *co-ordinating*, which become especially important when one
is dealing with subordinates who are themselves leaders of groups.
In addition on such courses much attention could be paid to the
theory and practice of both analytical and creative thinking, for
the leader's intellectual ability in these two spheres becomes
steadily more important as his responsibilities grow. Although
some progress has been made in the study of thinking and the
ways of developing clear and creative thought there can be little
doubt that much more research is both required and possible.[17]

At this level also, it is necessary that leaders should also understand much more about their responsibility for locating, releasing
and developing the leadership potential of those under them.
Besides practical group exercises, case-studies and observation of
films on these themes and others, a course at this stage—lasting
perhaps a week—could fruitfully include a higher content of
lectures on relevant topics.

The senior level of management, however, may also profit from
an advanced study of leadership at the summit of large organisations. Moreover, men and women in this category need to know
the concepts of leadership guiding their junior and middle
managers, both in order to know what is going on and also so

that they can employ a common language in which to pass on their experience and wisdom to their subordinates.

Summary

The corporate leadership in any large organisation goes by different names but the heart of it is always a response to the task, the team maintenance and the individual needs of the organization. In the services this corporate leadership goes by the name of 'Command'; in industry it is called 'Management'. The scientific techniques used by management are servants to the primary functions of leadership.

In order to develop such potential, here as elsewhere, it is important to take into account the five key areas of leadership training. Experiment in one of these—the provision of leadership courses—owes much to the Group Dynamics movement, which by its emphasis on small group work has pointed the way forward, but does not in itself supply the answer. More relevant courses focusing on the leadership element of managerial responsibility should take place on three main levels, with content and methods of education appropriate to them.

Lastly, it may be noted that the responsibility for the introduction of effective leadership training lies with the top level of management. To a British Institute of Management audience of senior managers in 1962 Lord Slim underlined the issue at stake :

There's more than opportunity for leadership, there's stark necessity for it. The men in the workshop and office today are the same, or of the same breed, as those who won the war. They are as ripe now as they were then for intelligent, understanding personal leadership—and they would rather be led than managed. 'Man management' is a horrible term and I'm ashamed that the army introduced it. Men like being led—not managed. This country has never failed to produce leadership when needed. It will not fail now to find the kind of leadership that puts life and meaning into management. There's a lot of it in this room now. There's more outside. Let's use it.[18]

CHAPTER EIGHT

LEADERSHIP TRAINING FOR
JUNIOR MANAGERS

In this chapter some experiments in applying the Sandhurst course in functional leadership to the needs of industry will be reviewed. In each case the author was approached by the top management of the firms or bodies concerned, and asked to devise and conduct courses based upon the model described above in Chapter 5. It should be stressed that these are experimental courses, and do not represent the 'finished article', but they illustrate the ways in which the content and methods of education advocated in this book can be as equally effective in industry and commerce as in the Armed Services.

Wates Limited

Wates Ltd. is a private company of building and civil engineering contractors with 4,000 employees. Upon hearing the author lecture at an Industrial Society management conference at Oxford in 1966 the Managing Director, Mr Neil Wates, asked him to make a 'feasibility study' to see whether or not the Sandhurst approach could be applied to the construction industry.

The author spent several days meeting employees of the firm at every level, from operatives on building sites to the company's directors, with three main aims in mind : (1) to look at the 'structure' of the firm from the leadership training point of view, (2) to determine how far and in what ways leadership entered into management responsibility in this industry, and (3) to find out how far a short course in functional leadership would be acceptable in the firm.

It soon became clear that the structure of the firm left little to be desired from the leadership training angle. Moreover, the author in conversations with a variety of men, some conducted while clutching his safety helmet in the wind on the tops of un-finished lofty tower blocks, established that the three areas of *task, team maintenance* and *individual needs* did indeed de-scribe the leadership responsibility of managers in this industry. Those he spoke to were unanimous in their awareness of the contrasts involved in working on building sites with different levels of productivity and morale, and all thought that the leader-ship of the site manager was an important factor in determining the difference. Finally, the reactions from the 'Executive Circle', a group of 100 key managers in the firm, to a lecture from the author left no doubts that this kind of training would be warmly welcomed by the company's senior management.

As a result of this study it was agreed that a series of three concentrated courses, each of one day's duration, would be run for the junior levels of management in the firm. Two of the Company's senior staff collaborated with the author in working out the details of the course described in Chapter 5, and its adaptation to the building industry. The plan was for the author to lead the first course and then gradually hand over to a Wates' senior executive responsible for management development. The immediate superiors of those taking part would be briefed on the aims and methods of the course, so that they could contribute to the follow-up training 'on the job'. Lastly, course members would be brought together three or four months later in order to evaluate the training in terms of how far it had helped them to be more effective both in their practice of leadership and in their observation of it.

Three one-day courses were held in the summer and autumn of 1967, each attended by fifteen young managers in their Section Manager, Site Agent positions or their equivalent in the Plant Yard or Head Office. For small group work each course was divided into three syndicates with appointed chairmen or leaders.

The programme began at 8.25 a.m. and lasted until 6.00 p.m. In its outlines it followed the functional leadership course de-scribed in Chapter 5. Apart from orientating the case-study to the construction industry, the main difference lay in Session 2, the Observation Exercise. Instead of the three practical tasks of the Armed Services courses, the pattern was as follows:

1. A practical outdoor group task along Armed Services lines but more complicated.

2. A group with a decision to make within time-limits, with all members except the chairman given a rôle to play.
3. A group with recommendations to make relevant to the industry, still within time-limits. Observers to act as consultants, two to each participant, at intervals throughout the task.

In the second two exercises the leader was seen in the role of chairman. In all three, of course, the emphasis was upon observation, enabling the course as a whole to make progress in observing the functions supplied—or omitted—in order to get the task done, hold the group together and meet individual needs. The inter-relations of the three areas and the degree of skill in the provision of functions also formed matters for comment by the observers. In order to help the observers to identify key functions they were issued with an Observation Sheet, based on the one evolved over several years at Sandhurst (see Appendix D). A short session on the factors involved in decision-making completed the morning's work.

After each session the course members evaluated it and also assessed the course as a whole at the end of the day, using the same scale and evaluation sheets as in the Army. The ratings were as follows:

Sessions	Poor 0	Average 40			Good 60			V. Good 80			Excellent 100			Average %		
		(1)	(2)	(3)	(1)	(2)	(3)	(1)	(2)	(3)	(1)	(2)	(3)	(1)	(2)	(3)
1. What is Leadership?	–	3	3	1	7	5	11	4	5	1	0	2	–	61	68	60
2. Observation Exercise	–	2	3	1	6	1	5	7	6	6	–	5	1	66	77	70
3. '12 O'Clock High'	–	1	2	1	3	3	1	9	5	8	2	4	3	76	75	80
4. Case-Study	–	–	1	–	6	1	5	6	6	8	3	7	–	76	85	72
5. Whole Course	–	–	–	–	5	3	3	8	9	9	2	3	1	76	80	76

Note: In some sessions one or two participants did not offer a rating.

1. WATES LTD. LEADERSHIP COURSE RATINGS

It should be stressed that course member reactions in the form of numerical ratings and comments, although a valuable yardstick, is only one of four possible criteria (see pp. 93–5 above). In the case of the three Wates Ltd. courses, however, they contributed to the final judgment that the project had been worthwhile from the points of view of the participants, the training staff and the company itself. This conclusion was confirmed by the 'follow-up' recapitulation sessions in London and Birmingham some months later, when it was clear that the young managers on the whole were still finding the course relevant to their day-to-day work, and also as a guide for their future development. Post-course reaction is even more difficult to assess, however, as the content and methods learnt on the course ought to become sub-conscious. But such recapitulation sessions (like reaction sheets on the course) not only serve as instruments for evaluation but also act as an educational method. They emphasise the value which the firm places on good leadership and remind all concerned that learning about it, by the nature of the subject, must be a continuing process throughout a man's career. Having completed the series of three courses in 1967 under the guidance of the author, Wates Limited have decided to run a further series each year under the direction of their own training staff.

Dorothy Perkins Ltd

As a result of a lecture delivered by the author to the Institute of Personnel Management's Annual Conference in 1966 he was asked whether or not the functional approach to leadership training could be applied to the development of the leadership potential of trainee branch manageresses in Dorothy Perkins Ltd., a public company with some 2,900 employees selling ladies' clothes in over 260 branches.

Again careful 'feasibility study' preceded the training course. In particular two senior and successful branch manageresses discussed with the author the functions which they performed to achieve both high sales and team spirit among their staff. Again the structure of the firm, an important dimension in leadership development, had to be taken thoroughly into account.

Sixteen young women between the ages of 18 and 25 years, all Junior Management Trainees, took part in the leadership course, which followed the original Sandhurst timings by being spread over two days. The practical part of the Observation Session 2 in this case consisted of changing a complicated window display at very short notice. There were two group tasks of this nature, and only one focusing upon leadership in the group meeting situation.

The session rating were as follows :

Sessions	Poor 0	Average 40	Good 60	V. Good 80	Excellent 100	Average %
1. What is Leadership	–	4	11	1	1	59
2. Observation Exercise	–	0	8	8	1	71
3. Decision-making	–	2	8	6	1	67
4. '12 O'Clock High'	–	1	5	10	0	71
5. Case-Study	–	0	3	12	1	77
6. Whole Course	–	1	3	12	0	73

2. DOROTHY PERKINS LTD. LEADERSHIP COURSE RATINGS

Again the comments of the participants both in the last session and also upon their 'Whole Course' evaluation sheets supported these ratings, as did the judgment of the senior managers involved in the course. It was planned that each trainee would be placed in temporary charge of a branch for at least a day shortly after this course, so that they could relate theory to practice. During the next part of their sandwich training at the company's head offices a recapitulation session on the functional leadership course allowed them to discuss their experiences 'in charge' in the light of the course. From all points of view this session confirmed the value of their earlier training in leadership. In addition the girls had learnt to observe the differences in leaders and to understand why one branch manageress was more effective than another.

Wilson (Connolly) Holdings Ltd.

As a consequence of a report in *The Financial Times* on the Wates Ltd. series of courses, the Chairman of Wilson (Connolly) Holdings Ltd. asked the author to conduct a similar course in his group of firms mostly concerned in the building industry and employing some 1,200 people.

A special feature of this course lay in the much older average age of those attending. Ages ranged from 22 years to 49 years, but ten out of the 15 course members were 35 years or over. It was felt that if men of considerable management experience underwent the course they would be both better able to evaluate its relevance for that particular group of firms and also—if it proved satisfactory—they would be able to judge who should be

132

selected for it. Owing to this more senior course membership the case-study was set at a higher level than usual. The ratings on the session evaluation sheets are given below :

Sessions	Poor 0	Average 40	Good 60	V. Good 80	Excellent 100	Average %
1. What is Leadership?	–	1	10	4	–	64
2. Observation Exercise	–	–	4	10	1	76
3. Decision-making	–	1	9	5	0	65
4. '12 O'Clock High'	–	1	5	8	1	72
5. Case-Study	–	–	1	11	3	82
6. Whole Course	–	–	2	12	1	78

3. WILSON (CONNOLLY) HOLDINGS LTD. LEADERSHIP
COURSE RATINGS

Although this course, as a pilot scheme, must be adjudged a success, it confirmed the author's belief that this particular form of functional leadership training requires at least two days and that it is most appropriate for younger men and women on the threshold of their management careers. The value which men of more advanced age and experience gain from it for their own work is of necessity limited, but their verdicts on the course from first-hand acquaintance can prove invaluable in assessing this approach for a particular industry. Also the participants may be better equipped to communicate with their younger staff about leadership and thereby to play a more effective part in the development of the firm's management potential.

The Industrial Society

The Industrial Society is an independent and self-financing body, founded in 1918. Its 5,500 members include industrial and commercial companies, nationalised industries, central and local government departments, employers' organisations and trade unions. At present the Society is particularly concerned with the development of effective leadership by manager and supervisors in works and offices, improved management/trade union relations, the evolution of conditions of employment appropriate to the requirements of modern jobs, adequate communication and the development of young employees. To these ends the

133

Society brings together more than 10,000 people each year on its courses, conferences and working discussions.

The Industrial Society decided to organise and run a number of functional leadership courses along the lines of the one devised by the author. The first experimental course in this series was held in November 1967. This occupied one day in the last of three weeks, each separated by several months, which form the Industrial Society's Modern Management Course. Consequently the course members—15 highly qualified middle level managers drawn from thirteen firms and representing a cross-section of British industry—had already had numerous lectures on social psychology, practical case studies and observation exercises. Despite this fact and the comparatively senior level of the participants, the course was rated highly by them.

As a result of the lessons learnt on this course the next in the series, held in March 1968, lasted for two days. Certain minor changes were made in the contents of the course at the planning stage, and in addition two innovations were made, one consisting of a lecture and discussion on 'The Motivation to Work', and the other a separate session on the 'qualities approach', illustrated by a Canadian Air Force film on 'Integrity'. The course was attended by 17 managers between the ages of 25 and 35 years, with some senior participant-observers making their number up to 20. In addition four management training specialists from several major companies sat in as observers. Their ratings on the sessions are included with those of the participants :

Session	Poor 0	Average 40	Good 60	V. Good 80	Excellent 100	Average %
1. What is Leadership?	–	11	11	2	–	54
2. Observation Exercise	–	2	8	13	1	70
3. '12 O'Clock High'	–	–	5	17	2	77
4. Case-Study	–	5	13	5	1	61
5. 'Motivation to Work'	–	1	1	17	5	81
6. 'Integrity' (film)	–	6	8	1	–	53
7. Whole Course	–	1	8	13	–	70

4. THE INDUSTRIAL SOCIETY LEADERSHIP COURSE NO. 2

The low ratings for the case-study, usually high, call for comment. On this occasion we attempted a complicated case-study involving a committee meeting which was interrupted by a telephone call bearing news of a sudden crisis which should have led the chairman to make a sudden change in the task of his group. Partly for technical reasons and partly because of inadequate briefing on the author's part this case-study went off at half-cock. One conclusion drawn from this exercise is that clear, simple and fairly short case-studies are the best in this sort of training.

The Canadian film on 'Integrity' also received low rating, not because members did not think the 'qualities approach' unimportant but because they felt that the film added little to what they already knew or had learnt on the preceding day. Dr Bill Paul's lecture on 'The Motivation to Work', in a session which focused on the 'Individual Needs' circle of the three interlocking areas of leadership responsibility, was particularily well received. Dr Bill Paul, now a consultant with I.C.I. lectured on the research work of Professor Herzberg in America, with whom he worked for a time, and also upon his own applications of Professor Herzberg's theory in the United Kingdom.

* * *

The following are some typical examples of comments by participants in answer to one of the questions on the final reaction sheet issued at the end of all the above courses, 'What have you, personally, learnt about leadership today?'

Leadership is a complex subject. I have found a framework to assess the performance of others and myself and I have learnt to be more aware and more observant.

That it is possible to evaluate one's own performance in leadership situations and develop one's own leadership ability.

That a balance between task, team maintenance and individual needs must be created.

And appreciation of the many qualities required. In my own case the need to delegate and thereby leave myself with more time to give to the more onerous aspects of the job.

135

The need to care for individuals and to explain the task as clearly as possible.

I have learnt to analyse clearly a problem in leadership.

That leadership has a pattern but that it is your personality that decides whether or not you make a success of your knowledge of this pattern.

The three circles outlined in the course, i.e. task, team maintenance and individual need are important whilst carrying out any task and any one of them being omitted may cause a failure to carry out the job.

A great deal—I did not realise so much was needed in leadership and this course has given me a number of points which I shall be able to remember.

I have found the Task/Team Maintenance/Individual Needs three circles a sound basis on which to focus my thinking in this field.

I have a completely different outlook on leadership and can now see why the managers I have admired are such good leaders and why some have failed. The most difficult part is yet to come, and yet I hope I have taken in the essentials of what I need to understand in order to make a good leader.

Conclusion

The adaptation of the functional leadership course to the needs of industry is still only in the experimental stage. Further changes in parts of it will no doubt have to be made, but enough has been written in this chapter at least to show that the broad approach has been well received both by the participants and the sponsoring firms or bodies. Certainly at the level of junior management training a functional leadership course had proved that it can be effective.

Many factors are involved in the success of such leadership training : the structure of the firm, the tutorial staff, the selection of the right course members, and the physical setting, to name only a few. Those who lead these courses should not be putting over a 'drill'; the content of it should be a living, growing part of their own thinking, kept up-to-date by contact with others responsible for such training. Given such favourable conditions there is plenty of evidence that functional leadership courses can make a specific and valuable contribution to the development of management potential.

CONCLUSION

This book contains the findings and conclusions of seven years' of research and experiment on the author's part into the subject of leadership training. Although this work originated in a military setting, it is relevant to training activities in industry, commerce and many other fields. Besides a number of firms, the management studies departments of several universities, a police college, a city fire service, local and municipal government offices, the Girl Guides movement, a national group of banks, a foreign country's Outward Bound Trust, a professional pilot's association and several churches are only some of the bodies in the United Kingdom and abroad who have shown a lively interest in the methods of developing leadership potential described in the preceding pages.

At this stage it needs perhaps to be re-iterated that 'one cannot teach leadership—it can only be learnt'. An educational situation can be created in which the students are able to make discoveries for themselves through group discussion and practical exercises. The ingredients in that situation need to be thought out carefully, so that the challenges that it poses are neither too easy nor too difficult. The responsibility for learning, however, rests upon the student. Therefore the title of this book—'Training for Leadership'—is partly a misnomer, unless it is taken to mean 'self-training'. It may be hoped that those who are using the book with such a purpose in mind will find the study of Chapter 2, in the light of Chapter 1, particularly profitable.

How much a participant receives from a leadership training course will depend ultimately upon how much he gives to it. This educational fact makes evaluation difficult, for the good student will tend to 'redeem' a bad syllabus, finding value in it hidden to others according to his need. He will learn, even if all he learns is more patience. Consequently student reaction must be regarded as only one of the possible criteria by which the success of training may be judged.

The current 'anti-leadership' ideas prevalent among many intellectuals and educationalists have been touched upon but not discussed in any depth in this book. For the most part these ideas rest upon false assumptions or misconceptions about the nature of leadership. Good leadership always exists in a form appropriate to its environment, and a shape which is fitting in one situation may not be so in another. Usually when people condemn leadership they are rejecting a particular image of it culled from a *milieu* different from their own.

The word 'good' has been used in connection with leadership in this book in the sense of proficiency rather than moral worth. A similar use of it is found in the New Testament sentence 'I am the good shepherd...', where the Greek word for 'good' means 'skilled in the craft' rather than good in the ethical sense. Yet it is perhaps not possible in an age which has seen the word 'leader' debased by its equivalent words in German and Italian, *Führer* and *Duce*, to avoid raising ethical questions in connection with a subject such as leadership training. Is the functional approach as described in these pages merely a cold method of analysing leadership and developing efficient but spiritually empty 'modern' leaders?

One way of replying to this question would be to say that leadership is a morally neutral phenomenon which takes on good or bad overtones from the task which the leader seeks to achieve in co-operation with his group. A moral 'end' justifies the leadership 'means'; an immoral one condemns its leader first and foremost.[1]

The author would go further than this view and suggest that ultimately the personal moral goodness of the leader does matter as well. This belief may be rationalised along certain lines. Perhaps most work is wasted, or at least of only temporal significance, soon seeping away into the estuary sands of time. But other objectives and aims link up and can be eventually related, like tributaries flowing into a river, to the purpose of mankind. If the vision of the end of that purpose is seen in personal terms then it becomes increasingly important that leaders should exemplify as far as they can the qualities which are necessary if mankind is to draw near to that goal. Central among these qualities is the reality we call goodness.

This view may be strengthened if we perceive 'opposing forces' at work to prevent mankind from achieving its purpose, to disrupt its unity, and to reduce or destroy the individual, three 'areas' which here—as upon every lesser human stage—interact upon each other for better or for worse. In this context such evidence as we have that goodness is *the* quality in human nature above all others durable against the assaults of evil in such situations as concentration camps, takes on a new significance.[2] Certainly 'integrity' and 'moral courage', the brother and sister of goodness, are often stressed as core qualities in the character of a good leader.[3]

Leadership, it may be added in conclusion, may often draw a man or woman into situations in which goodness will be tested by loneliness if by no stronger evil force. Perhaps only those leaders who pass through their ordeal, refined or tempered, can contribute anything of lasting value to the progress of mankind, or even to that of one other human soul.

APPENDIX A

Qualities of a Leader

US Marine Corps
Integrity
Knowledge
Courage
Decisiveness
Dependability
Initiative
Tact
Justice
Enthusiasm
Bearing
Endurance
Unselfishness
Loyalty
Judgment
(Card MCS Form
719)

RMC Canada
Loyalty
Professional
Competence
Courage
Honesty
Commonsense
Good Judgment
Confidence
Initiative
Tact

Self-Control
Humour
Personal Example
Energy
Enthusiasm
Perseverence
Decisiveness
Justice
(Syllabus 1962)

US Army
Bearing
Courage (Physical
and Moral)
Decisiveness
Endurance
Initiative
Integrity
Judgment
Justice
Loyalty
Tact
Unselfishness
(FM 22–100
Military
Leadership)

BRNC (Dartmouth)
Faith

Courage
Loyalty
Sense of duty
Integrity
Humanity
Commonsense
Good Judgment
Tenacity
Fortitude
Physical and
Mental Fitness
Self-Control
Cheerfulness
Knowledge
(BR 2138)

Judgment
Team Spirit
(Address to
RMAS July
1953)

RAF College
Efficiency
Energy
Sympathy
Resolution
Courage
Tenacity
Personality
(Amp 202)

FM Lord Harding
Fitness
Integrity
Courage
Initiative
Willpower
Knowledge

FM Lord Slim
Courage
Willpower
Initiative
Knowledge
(Address to RMAS
14 Oct 1953)

APPENDIX B

'Twelve O'Clock High'

1. The Film

'Should a wartime commander lead his men or drive them? Order them and tolerate no argument, or strive to persuade them? This is the age-old military dilemma which provides the theme for tonight's feature film, which has Gregory Peck as the new-broom C.O. appointed to rebuild a badly battered and morally shaken American bomber group stationed in England.

'Twelve O'Clock High' (the title refers to the rear-gunner's clock-code sighting report of an attacking enemy) was made in 1950 with Henry King, himself a former pilot, directing.

'Though about the war, it is not primarily an action picture; it is more concerned with the problems and lonely decision imposed by command, so the story is told principally in dialogue —very thoughtfully written dialogue—and the drama derives from the conflict of personalities.

'However, there is one excellent sequence of aerial warfare, and this is made up entirely of clips from newsreels.

'Supporting Peck as the martinet General Savage are Gary Merrill as the 'too-soft-with-the-men' Colonel Davenport whom he supplants, and Hugh Marlow as Colonel Ben Gately.'

(*Radio Times*, 23 March 1967)

2. The Historical Background

The film is set against a background of the United States Air Force in Britain during the Second World War, which was under the command of General Arnold.

The U.S.A. entered the Second World War at the end of 1941. Their forces came to Britain in mid-1942 to take part in the offensive against Germany and their main contribution was the

8th Air Force. The Bomber Command of the 8th Air Force was equipped with the B17 bomber, the famous Flying Fortress. This aircraft was heavily armed with 10 guns and was designed for daylight bombing. The R.A.F. had tried daylight bombing in 1939 but our day bombers were unsuitable and heavy losses made us switch to night bombing. The Americans still believed that they could make daylight bombing work and they pinned their hopes on the B17. The Bomber Command of 8th Air Force in Britain in 1942 had four groups, each group containing three squadrons. A group operated from one station and when it flew on a mission each of its three squadrons put up seven aircraft. The group flew in a tight box formation so that its 21 aircraft could bring 210 guns to bear on attacking enemy fighters. This film is about one group, the 918th bomb group operating from a station called Archbury.

The film, made when the war was fresh in people's memories, realistically portrays the kind of situations that the 8th Air Force did face in 1942 when trying to make daylight bombing work with raw inexperienced aircrew. The cost, however, became extreme. In the raid on Schweinfurt, the great ball bearing factory centre, of the 291 'Flying Fortress' in the raid 60 failed to return and 138 were badly damaged.

The ultimate solution was to be the development of a long-range fighter (the P51 Mustang) which could accompany the American bombers all the way to Germany. But until the extra bombers and fighters could be produced, the Americans had to rely upon leadership to make their policy work.

Twelve O'Clock High deals with the problems which faced the American bomber pilots in the early part of the war. The film goes on rather a long time, and the last forty minutes mainly concern the problem of 'combat fatigue', which is the reason why it is not shown on functional leadership courses.

144

APPENDIX C

Post-Sandhurst Evaluations

By the middle of 1967 officer cadets of Intakes 35 and 36 had been commissioned for two years, time enough for them to complete their specialist training courses and to have been platoon or troop commanders for a year or more. The Leadership Committee at Sandhurst decided to ask these young officers for their 'hindsight' assessment of the leadership training they had undergone at R.M.A.S. To this end a cross section of 100 young officers were sent a confidential questionnaire and asked to complete it.

This piece of research was very much in the nature of a 'pilot scheme' and it was designed not to yield statistical results but a general impression of how far the functional approach to leadership training had proved relevant 'on the job'. To have produced more quantative results a different questionnaire would have had to be issued, backed by interviews with the young officers themselves and with their commanding officers. Research of this kind, however, was not practicable, necessary through it may be judged.

The 70 replies received came from a complete cross-section of young officers in the modern army. The general impression gained from them was an encouraging one, namely that the leadership training at Sandhurst—both in its older and newer forms—had been highly beneficial, although many advanced constructive suggestions for its improvement. These conclusions can be illustrated by some quotations from the replies, prefaced by the writer's brigade, or corps, and whereabouts he had mainly served.

(1) *Brigade of Guards. Aden.*

'It is of course impossible to separate the leadership aspect of the syllabus from the rest. The whole course was aimed at producing leaders. The "Leadership Course" itself was well thought out, and we are all unlikely to forget the "3-circles" system.

'The Army does not work on the lines of a natural society. The officer is an artificial leader, imposed by the weight of his shoulder stars, until he had proved himself the real leader, that is until he has learnt what functions should be supplied, and how he should carry them out.

[The writer took command of a platoon of guardsmen of another regiment who had already been in Aden for a year. Gradually he built up mutual respect with his men. He found it difficult to analyse how he achieved this, but gave some examples]

'We had trouble in my platoon with carrying G.P.M.G's [General Purpose Machine Guns] on night patrols. So when I took a G.P.M.G. on another officer's patrol I learned a lot.

'We had to build three sangars [low walls] around a well site. I supervised the over-all siting and building of the three, but I was principally concerned with one, my platoon sergeant with another, and a section commander with the other. Once everything was sorted out I started to fill sand bags by my sangar. After half-an-hour the platoon sergeant and section commander began to fill sandbags also. I had said nothing to them about doing so. The result : three good sangars built in record time (in 100°F.), with the platoon exhausted but happy. I had done what I felt was most useful. Incidentally, it made an enormous difference to platoon morale to return to camp, under the eyes of a number of interested, varied and quite senior spectators with Sir quite as dirty as the filthiest guardsman.'

(2) *Welsh Brigade. Cyprus (with United Nations forces) and B.A.O.R.*

'Whilst I was at the R.M.A. the actual teaching of leadership was in a new experimental stage. However, having been introduced to the latest philosophies on the subject, as opposed to a list of qualities against which one could assess oneself, it is now possible on occasions to make a "leadership appreciation". In particularly in terms of the task needs, team maintenance and the individual needs, to quote the precis.

'*Example:* Lately, a considerable amount of my time has been spent instructing soldiers of different grades from the recruit to the N.C.O., and by the simple application of the above (task needs etc.) in the form of a question to myself, both indoor and outdoor lessons and exercises have been improved.

'After some time one is no longer making a conscious effort to adhere to these principles as they become a part of the sub-conscious logical thought-process during the preparation and running of the lesson ...

'At the R.M.A. the "walls" of leadership are provided but it is up to the individual to "roof" these foundations with his own principles, standards and methods. I feel that self-analysis during the early days of one's regimental career is no bad thing. Many practical and theoretical examples of "do's" and "dont's" from the R.M.A. but a few minutes in thought each evening reflecting on the days work would ensure that each young officer provided himself with a sound "roof". This is particularly so for the Infantry Officer where the leadership is very direct. His men are led by his words, his actions and his example.'

(3) *Royal Engineers. United Kingdom.*

'It was of great value in that it made me think about the subject and crystallise one's thoughts during the course ...

'At present I have just taken over a bridge-building task in Scotland. Morale has considerably improved since I completed an overall plan; the three areas in leadership having been filled.'

(4) *Parachute Brigade. Bahrain, Trucial States, Aden and Kenya.*

'Leadership training at Sandhurst falls into the natural categories of theory and practice. By the time a cadet leaves R.M.A.S. he has a very sound knowledge of the theory from organised discussions, lectures and the study of military history. The cadet receives practical training in leadership through the carrying out of his senior term appointments and his handling of his fellow cadets in the field ... I found, however, during my time in the Middle East that the basic grounding in leadership received at R.M.A.S. was invaluable.'

(5) *Royal Army Ordnance Corps. Training Depot, United Kingdom.*

'I believe that leadership training is terribly important, especially today, and that all the leadership training I did was not wasted. The difficulty is convincing an over-confident cadet just how important (and difficult) good leadership and man-management is!

'Finally I should like to mention that I have served under two Commanding Officers since I was commissioned, one of whom was generally considered good, and the other who is, with all due respect, considered "not so good". Under the latter I think I have learnt even more than under the former. I now know how galling it is to be badly handled, and I think that this has helped me in my own approach to leadership.'

(6) *Fusilier Brigade. United Kingdom.*

'At Sandhurst much depended on the individual making his *own* attempt to "grow in stature". The functional approach was extremely relevant. It is a guide to be used when personal feelings come to the fore. The phrase "over identification with one's men" [a phrase from the film *Twelve O'Clock High*] covers what I have found to be the most difficult part of leadership.'

(7) *Royal Military Police. United Kingdom.*

'I have found that the functional approach has been a first class foundation upon which to build my own technique of leadership.'

(8) *Royal Corps of Signals. Singapore and Borneo.*

'I would like to see the actual leadership syllabus spread out over the whole course with much exhortation to think about it. It really should be driven home to cadets that this, above all else, will have to be practised within weeks of leaving R.M.A.S. If a cadet makes a mess of his leadership in the opening few weeks of his first job then the whole of his first posting is likely to be ruined. He will learn the hard way, but he may have to wait for $2\frac{1}{2}$ years before he gets a new job and therefore a new chance to put it into practise the lessons he has taught himself!'

(9) *Royal Corps of Transport. B.A.O.R.*

'This side of leadership has proved extremely relevant. Being a transporter one is faced with many problems ... which are not able to be studied at Sandhurst or the Junior Officer's Course after the R.M.A. The functional approach, however, enables one to overcome any extraordinary problems.'

(10) *Royal Armoured Corps. United Kingdom.*

'Subconsciously the functional approach to leadership has

influenced me quite a lot, although at the time it would appear that one doesn't take a lot of notice of "Team Maintenance", "Individual Needs" etc.'

(11) *Royal Artillery. B.A.O.R.*
'The leadership training gave us a very good foundation on which to build from the practical experience received as a commissioned officer ... Sandhurst, I am certain, has a system that allows mistakes to be made where they can be corrected without making the soldiers suffer and to the benefit of the leader.'

(12) *Royal Engineers. Aden.*
'The functional approach to leadership helped me to have a form to my leadership. As a result of the course I had a general picture of the relationship I should aim at with my soldiers.'

APPENDIX D

OBSERVATION SHEET

FUNCTION	COMMENTS

PLANNING

e.g. Seeking all available information
     Defining group task, purpose or goal
     Making a workable plan (in right
     decision-making framework)

INITIATING

e.g. Briefing group on the aims and the
     plan
     Explaining *why* aim or plan is necessary
     Allocating tasks to group members
     Setting group standards

CONTROLLING

e.g. Maintaining group standards
     Influencing tempo
     Ensuring all actions are taken
     towards objectives
     Keeping discussion relevant
     Prodding group to action/decision

SUPPORTING

e.g. Expressing acceptance of persons
     and their contribution
     Encouraging group/individuals
     Disciplining group/individuals
     Creating team spirit
     Relieving tension with humour

Reconciling disagreements or getting
others to explore them

INFORMING
e.g. Clarifying task and plan
Giving new information to the group
i.e. keeping them 'in the picture'
Receiving information from group
Summarising suggestions and ideas
coherently

EVALUATING
e.g. Checking feasibility of an idea
Testing the consequences of a proposed
solution
Evaluating group performance
Helping the group to evaluate its
own performance against standards

NOTES AND BIBLIOGRAPHY

Chapter 1. *The Nature of Leadership*

1. C. Bird, *Social Psychology* (D. Appleton-Century, New York London, 1940) pp. 378–379. Professor Bird of the University of Minnesota looked at approximately 20 studies 'bearing some resemblance to controlled investigations' which contained 79 traits. 'Surprisingly little overlapping is found from study to study. Actually, 51 or 65 per cent, are mentioned once, 16 or 20 per cent are common to two lists, 4 or 5 per cent are found in three, and another 5 per cent in four lists. Two traits are common to five lists, and one trait, namely initiative, to six, and another one, high intelligence, to ten lists.' (p. 379)

2. G.W. Allport and H.A. Odbert, 'Trait-names : A Psycholexical Study' *Psychological Monographs*, No. 211 (1936).

3. R. M. Stogdill, 'Personal Factors Associated with Leadership : A Survey of the Literature' *Journal of Psychology*, Vol. 25 (1948), pp. 35–71.

4. W. O. Jenkins, 'A Review of Leadership Studies with Particular Reference to Military Problems' *Psychological Bulletin*, Vol. 44 (1947), pp. 54–79.

5. A. H. Maslow, *Motivation and Personality* (Harper and Brothers, New York, 1954). The diagram appears in CFP 131 (2) *Leadership for the Professional Officer*, a Canadian Forces publication.

6. On the subject of motivation, closely related to the satisfaction of individual needs in work, the research work of F. Herzberg, Professor of Psychology at Western Reserve University, U.S.A. and his associates, is highly relevant. See F. Herzberg, B. Mausner and B. B. Snyderman, *The Motivation to Work* (2nd ed. John Wiley & Sons, New York, 1959). and F. Herzberg,

Work and the Nature of Man (World Publishing Co., Cleveland, 1966). Miss Lisl Klein, a research worker in industrial sociology, has written a thought-provoking pamphlet on the subject, *The Meaning of Work* (The Fabian Society, 1963). Dr J. H. Oldham's essay entitled *Work in Modern Society* (S.C.M. Press, 1950), is the best introduction to the theological understanding of work.

7. R. Tannenbaum and W. H. Schmidt, 'How to Choose a Leadership Pattern' *Havard Business Review,* March-April (1958).
8. R. Tannenbaum and W. H. Schmidt, *op. cit.*
9. C. A. Gibb, 'Leadership' *Handbook of Social Psychology* Vol. 2, ed. G. Lindzey (1954).

Further reading :
B. M. Bass, *Leadership, Psychology and Organizational Behaviour* (Harper & Row, New York, 1960). The author, Professor of Psychology at Louisana State University, discusses many of the 1,115 books and articles on leadership and cognate subjects listed in his Bibliography. An introduction to American research.
M. G. Ross and C. E. Hendry, *New Understandings of Leadership* (Association Press, New York, 1957). A clear discussion of the main theories about leadership and some of the research upon it.

Chapter 2. *Looking at Leaders*
J. M. Scott, *Gino Watkins* (Hodder & Stoughton, London, 1935).
Field Marshal Lord Slim, *Defeat into Victory* (Cassell, London, 1956).
J. A. C. Brown, *The Social Psychology of Industry* (Penguin Books, London, 1954).
Lieut. General Sir Brian Horrocks, *A Full Life* (Collins, London, 1960).
T. E. Lawrence by his Friends, ed. A. W. Lawrence (Jonathan Cape, London, 1937).

Further leadership case-studies may be found in the following books :
Paul Brickhill, *Reach for the Sky* (Collins, London, 1954). Includes description of the means used by Squadron Leader Douglas Bader (as he then was) to transform the morale of a Canadian Squadron back from Dunkirk.

Air Chief Marshal Sir Basil Embry, *Mission Accomplished* (Methuen, London, 1957) pp. 239–260. An account of his actions after taking command of 2nd Tactical Air Force in May 1943

T. T. Paterson, *Morale in War and Peace* (Parrish, London, 1955). The author, now Professor of Industrial Administration at the University of Strathclyde, served as a radar controller on an R.A.F. Station during the war and acted as a 'consultant' on morale problems to the Commanding Officer. The book illustrates graphically *inter alia* the relationship between 'task' and 'team maintenance'. A redefined aim restored unity between ground and air crews.

C. Woodham Smith, *Florence Nightingale* (Constable, London, 1950), pp. 152–25. The classic account of Miss Nightingale's work during the Crimean War.

G. C. Homans, 'The Small Warship' *American Sociological Review,* XI (1946), pp. 294–300. Professor of Sociology at Harvard University and an authority on the social psychology of small groups, G. C. Homans served in the U.S. Navy as a captain during the Second World War, and described in this article and factors which contribute to high morale at sea.

Chapter 3. *Leadership Selection*

1. H. Harris, *The Group Approach to Leadership Testing* (Routledge & Kegan Paul, London, 1949). The author started work with W.O.S.B. in 1943 and was still engaged upon them in later 1946 when he wrote his book.

2. A. Arnold-Brown, *Unfolding Character: The Impact of Gordonstoun* (Routledge & Kegan Paul, London, 1962), p. 81. As a captain the author served as an instructor at the Highland Fieldcraft Training Centre.

3. *Outward Bound,* ed. D. James (Routledge & Kegan Paul, London, 1957).

Chapters 4 and 5. *Leadership Syllabus*

Further reading for the specialist :

M. L. Johnson Abercrombie, *The Anatomy of Judgment* (London, 1960). Describes the use of the small group in developing more scientific ways of thinking among medical students.

J. Klein, *Working with Groups: The Social Psychology of Discussion and Decision* (Hutchinson, London, 1961). Some significant remarks on the nature of theory in social psychology (e.g. p. 25).

M. B. Miles, *Learning to Work in Groups. A Program Guide for Educational Leaders* (Teacher's College, Columbia University, New York, 1959). An American approach to leadership training, with annotated Bibliography.

Chapter 6. *Field Leadership Training*

1. *Defence Psychology.* ed. F. Geldard (Pergamon Press, London, 1962). See also, T. O. Jacobs, *A Program of Leadership Instructions for Junior Officers.* (The George Washington University Human Resources Research office and U.S. Army Infantry Human Research Unit, Fort Benning Georgia, 1963). Includes a full bibliography on this research and training programme (p. 21).

Chapter 7. *Leadership Training in Industry*

1. Lt. Col. D. M. Ramsay, U.S. Army, in 'Management or Command?' *Military Review*, Sept. 1961, makes this point clearly.

2. *Industrial Relations* (The Industrial Society, 1966). A pamphlet based on the experience of member organisations of The Industrial Society and written by Michael Clarke, then its Assistant Director and now general manager of industrial relations of the British Steel Corporation.

3. *Theories in Social Psychology,* ed. M. Deutsch and R. H. Krauss (Basic Books Inc. New York and London, 1965), last chapter.

4. J. A. C. Brown, *The Social Psychology of Industry.* (Penguin Books, London 1954). See also E. Mayo, *The Human Problems of an Industrial Civilization* (Macmillan, Boston, 1946, 2nd. ed.) for the Hawthorne experiments.

5. J. A. C. Brown, *op. cit.* pp. 77–78.

6. These qualities may perhaps be divided into the following categories : (a) those which describe tendencies to perform certain functions, e.g. 'initiative' (which can be related to 'initiating' action in groups), (b) qualities which can clearly be acquired or developed, e.g. confidence, (c) personality or temperamental traits, e.g. intelligence, and (d) core qualities of character, e.g. integrity, moral courage, and a sense of responsibility.

155

7. From *Making Leadership in Industry Effective,* a MS shortly to be published as a pamphlet, based upon a large number of lectures given to management audiences. For a valuable discussion of the 'Span of Control' concept, see R. Stewart, *The Reality of Management* (Heinemann, London, 1961) pp. 31–35. This book forms a first class general introduction to the problems of 'structure' in organisations, and industry in particular, with a useful Select Bibliography attached. For an American recognition of the importance of 'structure' in leadership training, see A. S. Tannenbaum, *Social Psychology of the Work Organization* (Wadsworth Publishing Co., California and Tavistock Publications, London, 1966) p. 83 *et. al.* See also M. Ivens, *The Practice of Industrial Communication* (Business Publications Ltd., London, 1963).

8. 'Group dynamics began as an identifiable field of enquiry in the United States towards the end of the 1930's. Its origination as a distinct speciality is associated primarily with Kurt Lewin (1890–1947) who popularized the term 'group dynamics'; made significant contributions to both research and theory in group dynamics, and in 1945 established the first organization devoted explicitly to research in group dynamics, 'Origins of Group Dynamics,' p. 9, in *Group Dynamics: Research and Theory* ed. D. Cartwright and A. Zander (Row, Peterson, New York, 1956. Tavistock Publications, London, 1960).

9. L. F. Urwick, 'Management in Human Relations' in R. Tannenbaum, I. R. Weschler, F. Massarik, *Leadership and Organization: A Behavioral Science Approach* (McGraw-Hill, New York, 1961), p. 421.

10. J. N. Fairhead, D. S. Pugh and W. J. Williams, *Exercises in Business Decisions. A Manual for Management Education* (E.U.P. London, 1965), p. 13. For signs that the Group Dynamics movement in Canada is recognising this weakness and evolving accordingly towards more emphasis on task-work, see Professor W. J. Reddin (University of New Brunswick) 'Training to a "T"' *Personnel Magazine,* (August, 1967).

11. H. B. Miles, *op. cit.,* p. 19.

12. *Leadership and Motivation. Essays of Douglas McGregor,* ed. W. G. Bennis and E. H. Schein (The M.I.T. Press, Cambridge Mass. and London, 1966). See also D. McGregor, *The Human Side of Enterprise* (Mcgraw-Hill, New York, 1960).

13. William H. Whyte, Jr. *The Organization Man* (Simon & Schuster, New York, 1955; Jonathan Cape, London, 1957).
14. In 1966 it was estimated that at least 100,000 people had been through Group Dynamics courses in the United States and the number is steadily increasing. For its progress in Europe, see G. Whitaker, *T-Group Training: Group Dynamics in Management Education* (The Association of Teachers of Management. Occasional Papers 2, Blackwell, Oxford, 1965).
15. See for example, R. Gosling, D. H. Miller, P. M. Turquet, D. Woodhouse, *The Use of Small Groups in Training* (The Codicote Press, 1967).
16. In my opinion the description of the opening minutes of a Group Dynamics group on pages 58 and 59 of A. K. Rice, *Learning for Leadership* (Tavistock Publications, 1965) illustrates this point.
17. The military approach to clear thinking known as 'Appreciations' forms a useful starting point from which to explore such methods as Critical Path Analysis. The University of Manchester is at present compiling a Bibliography on 'creativity'.
18. The Seventh Elbourne Memorial Lecture, 'Leadership', *The Manager* (Jan. 1962).

Conclusion

1. The following passage is an example of this reasoning:
'Leadership can be judged good or bad only in terms of goals ... Leadership in a democratic society offered by those who set worth on the individual should have as its goal helping people to be better people and the society to be a better society ... and should use only methods that are consistent with this goal. This means that good democratic leadership is essentially *educative* leadership. To be good leadership ... must be particularly clear in its vision of the goal and particularly scrupulous in its selection and use of methods. Leadership ... must respect the purposes and personalities of the members of the group. At the same time, it must steer towards the mere general goal that is involved.' R. J. Blakely, *Strategies of Leadership* (Harper, New York, 1959).
2. For the 'survival value' of character in wartime, see Lord Moran, *The Anatomy of Courage* (Constable, London, 2nd ed. 1966), and A. Farrar-Hockley, *The Edge of the Sword* (Frederick Muller, London, 1954), an account of the author's

experiences as a prisoner-of-war in Korea. For studies of civilian leaders in German prisons or concentration camps in the Second World War, see, for example, Dietrich Bonhoeffer, *Letters and Papers from Prison* (S.C.M. Press, London, 1959), *Dying We Live,* ed. H. Golliwitzer, K. Kuhn, and R. Schneider, trans. R. Kuhn (Fontana Books, London, 1958); and Comte Pierre d'Harcourt, *The Real Enemy* (Longmans, London, 1967).